WHITE BUTTERFLY

While parents minister,

a beloved daughter

disappears off the face

of the earth

VANDA TERRELL

✝HANNIBAL BOOKS
www.hannibalbooks.com

TO ORDER ADDITIONAL COPIES, SEE PAGE 207

Dedicated
to

The Lord.
May You continue to fill me with Living Water.

Acknowledgements

Our story took a while to unfold. In February 2005 God put on my heart the desire to share my journey with others. Through His power and guiding hand *White Butterfly* was born. Many people aided me in this process. First I give praise to my **heavenly Father.** Thanks to my husband, **Mike**, for loving me and standing with me for more than 30 years. Thank you to my daughter, **Brittany**, for allowing me to share our story. My son, **Chris**, has remained faithful and loving with his support. I am so blessed to have a son with such a caring spirit and an undying love for his sister. I often called my parents, **Brian and Margaret Hester**, to seek encouragement; I was always met with patience and a listening ear. Through my journey countless **colleagues at Plano Senior High School** read part or all of my manuscript and gave me valuable feedback. Special thanks goes to **Debbie Lindley** for proofing pages with a loving spirit. My **students at PSHS** lived this process with me, so a shout out goes to **Mrs. T's English classes of 2005-2006 and 2006-2007**. Thanks to **Sally Ray**, librarian at Plano Senior High School. She aided me in the editing process and led me to Hannibal Books. **Pastor Randy Bailey** of Four Corners Church in Plano, TX, was a true shepherd and stood with Mike and me through this process. He was always just a phone call away. Our **friends at Four Corners Church** loved us when we were broken and needed a shoulder on which to cry. Mike and I forever will be grateful to **Mike Guidry** for finding Brittany with the special care of a father. He is a man of integrity. **Louis and Kay Moore** deserve a special show of gratitude for believing in *White Butterfly* and its message. They are a true representation of Christian publishing. Thank You, **most gracious heavenly Father**, for loving me, molding me, and never giving up on me. He is so faithful.

Contents

Foreword

After reading the final pages of this amazing book, all I could do was to pray, "Lord Jesus, give me the grace to love those closest to me with your love every minute of every day."

Being the father of six children (five of them girls), I could not help but wonder, *What if one of my precious children was taken? What if one of my daughters was taken? What would I do? Where would I turn?*

As I read chapter by chapter, I was flooded by memories of my own personal and family tragedies while we served overseas in the former Soviet Union. When tragedy struck, I never will forget feeling so hopeless and helpless while being so far from home, from family, from friends, from resources— even from a familiar language. Suffering personally is one thing. Seeing your kids suffer is another. I felt for the Terrells in their tragedy with their daughter in such a faraway land.

This book is an amazing, intense, honest, heart-wrenching, and captivating story of tragedy to triumph. Once I started reading, I couldn't stop.

Most importantly, this book is a great reminder that sometimes the greatest blessings stem from the greatest pain. At least one of those great blessings is the rediscovery that God loves us more than we can ever fathom, no matter the circumstances of life. Read this book; you will not be disappointed.

Dr. Steve Hunter
Dean of Students, Criswell College, Dallas, TX
Associate Professor of Counseling and Psychology
Former Missionary to Central and Eastern Europe
Author, *Make-Believers*

What others are saying about this book:

White Butterfly is a poignant account of a mother's abiding, deep love for her child. Yet in the midst of heartbreak, sorrow, betrayal, and lies, good still triumphs over evil. Hope is never lost.

Mary Casey, Librarian, Plano Senior High School, Plano, TX

This book is about the courageous journey and the struggles Vanda and Mike Terrell encountered along the road of their missionary service. It paints a beautiful picture of parents' love, the great sacrifices they made to fight for their daughter, and the heartache that stems from disappointment. Fasten your seat belt, strap yourself in, and hang on for the ride!

Lauren Gillin, Educational Consultant, Electronic Data Systems, Plano, TX

Fantastic read! I couldn't wait to turn to the next page. It shows that love triumphs, especially in the face of fear, doubt, and questioning God, family, and friends! The book is truly riveting, but even with all the heartache, God's promise of "Love never fails" shines through all of the darkness.

Pete Kralyevich, Associate Pastor, Four Corners Church, Plano, TX

Vanda Terrell describes events that read like the plot of a detective novel. As they happened several years ago, I was aware of these very events through friends and through the news media. Now I am privileged to have met Vanda and to read the rest of the story. Just as dramatic as these events is Vanda's own awakening to the truth about her daughter. This book will touch all readers, especially Christian parents of prodigal children.

Sally Ray, Librarian, Plano Senior High School, Plano, TX

Vanda Terrell's unbelievable experience shows how endurance, forgiveness, and trust in God bring rewards in His perfect timing. Every parent who reads this book will be blessed and will learn to cherish every moment spent with their children and to never ever give up on them nor on God.

Linda Dean, MEd., Trauma and Loss School Specialist, Arlington, TX

Chapter 1

God's Call, or a Wrong Number?

As I lay quietly in bed, hoping for rest and peace, quiet, soft, small feet ventured down the carpeted stairs, through the kitchen, and into my bedroom. Instinctively I opened my eyes. Large, dark eyes met mine as I heard, "Mema, I had a bad dream."

Waking from a groggy sleep, I grumbled, "It's okay, Marie Lou. Let's go back upstairs. Mema will put you to bed."

As we climbed the staircase, Marie Lou asked, "Will you rub my tummy, please?"

"Sure, I will," I whispered as I stroked her ebony hair. My little angel climbed into bed and quickly fell fast asleep. *Now, if I could just be so lucky.*

Lying in bed and waiting for sleep to resume, my mind rapidly ran through the changes in our lives during the past 18 months. In just more than a year, Mike and I have become parents again. We are rearing our two granddaughters—Marie Lou, 5, and April, 4. Our lives are no longer our own. We have rearranged our home and our schedules and restructured our relationship to accommodate these two precious granddaughters. They have been with us almost 24/7 since Brittany's return.

Brittany's return . . . if you could call it that. For so long Mike and I prayed that we would find our daughter that we never imagined any ending except a happy one. However, I'm old enough to know that fairy tales are the only places in which happy endings can be found. Most often life gives us heartache.

Heartache and heartbreak—we know them well. Our beloved Brittany disappeared off the face of the earth while we served as missionaries in Mexico in 2000. Images of Brittany and the girls' father, Aldo, crowd my mind. *And now . . . now we are rearing two children who were brought into this world as a result of lies and deception. What will I say when these precious girls ask me, "Where's my daddy? Where was I born?"*—questions I dread answering.

What shall I say? "Well, let's see . . . your dad hid your mommy from us until she fell in love with him"?

Some might say that Aldo raped Brittany. She was, after all, only 15, and too young to legally consent, according to U.S. laws. But in Mexico, laws are different. Actions such as this are seldom if ever punished. What a nightmare!

Thank God that won't be a conversation I'll be having with my granddaughters any time soon, or at least, I hope not.

As I attempt to calm my mind, it travels back to a time in which Mike and I—along with Brittany—were excited about starting a new life in a new country. My mind has traversed that road many times as I try to trace the trail of events so I can pinpoint the exact moment at which everything began to unravel and fall apart. Though my memories are somewhat hazy, I clearly remember excitement—the excitement of a new adventure, of a new life, serving God in a new land: Mexico, in the beautiful, remote community of Bacalar. Bacalar, in the Yucatan Peninsula, is situated about 30 kilometers from the northern border of Belize. Bacalar is nestled next to the Laguna de Seite Colores, known as The Lake of Seven Colors.

The Laguna de Seite Colores is perhaps the most spectacular lake in the world. The name of the body of water is derived from the multi-faceted, blue colors of the water. Situated in Quintana Roo, Mexico, it is a place that is as far removed from civilization as one might imagine. No electricity, little water, animals running in and out of houses—a real Mayan community that time forgot. This was to be our new home. God had a plan for the Terrell family. That was the year 2000. My husband, Mike, and I, along with Brittany, sold just about everything we owned except the clothes on our backs and moved to this isolated region of Mexico.

When people think of Mexico, sometimes they instantly envision the exotic resort area of Cancun. Transferring to a place such as Cancun certainly would prompt thoughts of excitement. But this *pueblito,* or small village, was four hours removed from commercialized Cancun and all its splendor. The village of Bacalar has remained one of the last surviving Mayan communities. The indigenous people live in thatch huts with earthen floors and tattered curtains that replace doors and windows. Turkeys run like rainwater through the small, dirt houses. Small boys of 9 or 10 stand on the street corner and drink beer while others ride through the streets on bikes as they haul water or groceries for their families' dinners. Here husbands beat their wives and spank their children so hard all the neighbors can hear. In Bacalar, people have no secrets— except from the Anglos.

I had prayed for God's call for just the right place for our family to serve as missionaries. But Mexico? *Did I hear you right, Lord? Please, God, send us any where but Mexico! I don't even like Mexicans; moreover, I'm afraid of them!*

My mind wandered back to the fateful weekend on which this particular terror began—the weekend in which I was 14-years old and on a church-sponsored trip to Galveston Beach. After several hours of building sandcastles, playing volleyball, and sunning ourselves, my friend, Joanne, and I decided to walk down the boardwalk to show off our tans and our new bikinis. The wet, moist air smelled of salt, driftwood, and decaying garbage.

After walking for at least an hour, we determined that we needed to head back to the group, but we had gone too far— we were exhausted. A filthy, white Good Times van pulled up. The driver leaned out and asked us if we wanted a ride. This was the type of van my dad had always warned me about. Now it was right in front of me. The driver appeared to be about 20, wore mirrored sunglasses, and had scruffy, blond hair.

Joanne, who was much braver than I, said, "Sure, that sounds great!"

Bravely I attempted, "If you could just drop us off way down there by the second pier, that would be terrific!"

"Hop in," he said.

When the van door opened, I knew we were in trouble. Six Mexican men stared at me as they pulled us into the vehicle. The grimy, white van turned around and began heading the other direction, away from our safe, little youth group.

The darkness hid the clandestine adventure that awaited me. All the seats long ago had been removed and replaced with faded, gold shag carpet. It smelled musty. A cloud of cigarette smoke lingered in the air.

Moments went by. I tried to remain calm. A very large dark man sat in the far back of the van. A voice from the shadows told me to go sit by him. Through the darkness I could see his mouth crusted over in the corners where food still remained. A large, dark belly hung over his waist. His black beard curled around his face and up around his putrid mouth. The smell of tequila and cigarettes permeated his body, which scared me to death.

Speaking to me in Spanish and licking his lips, he looked at my young, firm body. My heart almost pounded out of my chest. Staring at me, he opened his mouth and began to stick out his tongue and asking me if I wanted a piece of ice. I said

"No" as politely as I could, but another dark man came up from behind me and put me in the large Mexican's lap.

As I sat in his lap and trembled with fear, I was forced to snuggle up to his hairy, dark chest, which smelled of sweat. He smiled. Tears pooled in my eyes as I was forced to take a piece of ice from his mouth. This became a game for the Buddha-looking, bare-chested man. I must have taken enough ice from his wretched mouth to fill a glass.

The van stopped. I noticed that we were on a deserted stretch of the beach. The quiet deafened my ears. I longed for laughter and sandcastles lining the beach.

No one was around anywhere. My friend, Joanne, who had been sitting up front with the driver and another man, abandoned me to go smoke a joint and left me in the van.

Thanks a lot, Joanne, I thought. *Now what?* I tried to remain calm. *She'll be back soon. Then we will be on our way.* I waited. The men spoke Spanish as they looked at my almost naked body with anticipation. One of the guys got out a knife and began twirling the blade on the palm of his hand. He looked at me with wanton, lusty eyes. He laid the blade on my thigh while he whispered to me in Spanish in a deep, husky voice. The blade twirled around on my sun-browned skin and glistened in the shadowy darkness. Loud Mexican music blared from the speakers, so I knew no one could hear me scream.

While one man caressed my long, blonde hair, the man with the knife slid the blade under the string that tied my bathing-suit bottoms together. My blood ran colder than the knife. I felt a tug. Then, as I looked down, my hips were exposed. I pleaded with the men to leave me alone.

My mind raced with horrid thoughts. *Are they going to kill me?* I wondered. *My body will be thrown into the ocean, never*

13

to be found. I wanted to run, but the men surrounded me on all sides. *What if I never see my parents again? They would never know what happened to me.*

I began to tremble; fear filled my spirit. "Where's Joanne?" I managed with a quivering lip.

One of the men said, "On the beach getting high. She's a lot more fun than you." He grinned and exposed several gold teeth. He leaned into me and salivated as he undressed me with his eyes.

Overcome with terror, I began to weep softly. At that moment, one of the men moved up from behind and untied the top of my bikini. My fate had been decided, I would be just another treasure for these wicked men who would hurt me and then discard me. I hugged my knees into my chest and prayed. "Oh, God," I pled with every bone in my body; "get me out of here . . . alive."

I will never know this side of heaven why things happened as they did. But these terrible men either had a change of heart, or God answered my prayer, or both, because at that very moment the van door opened. The men shoved me outside to join Joanne, who suddenly had appeared beside the van. From inside the smoke-filled van, I was handed a tattered and torn T-shirt to cover up my naked body. We rapidly made our way back to join the church group. Once back, I grabbed my cover-up and hoped no one would see me shaking.

For almost 20 years I never spoke to anyone about this incident. I felt ashamed and frightened, as if the whole incident had somehow been my fault. I suppressed all memory, all fear, all hurt. These emotions went deep inside my spirit and resided for many years. Despite my best efforts, the fear and the pain did not stay hidden but surfaced as a paralyzing force, which prohibited me from interacting with an entire people group. I became afraid of people of Latino descent and lived through many nightmares in which the large Mexican man taunted me with ice.

Needless to say, a miracle was required in order for me to be able to work with the Mayans in Mexico. So when God said *Mexico*, I was shaken, to say the least. This fear of the Latino culture had only festered under the surface. Until we received our assignment to Bacalar, I never realized how deep the resentment went.

But God can make even the most deep-seated resentment disappear. While I walked my dog one day, I prayed and asked God to deal with my fear and take it away. As soon as the words were spoken, the fear dissipated. At that very moment an oppressive spirit that had held me down for decades disappeared—all because I asked.

God healed the hurt that day. He lifted my fear. He was sending me to minister in Mexico. Who could say "No" to God? Not me! Even given the pain that we ultimately suffered, I would do it all again if He asked. What kind of Christian would I be if I said "No" to God?

As we received the Bacalar assignment, we saw it as a noble missionary opportunity: to open a school and a clinic for unwanted and abandoned children in the area of this remote part of Mexico. Mike and I believed it was God's calling. Both of us were sure it was what we were meant to do. While we both loved our comfortable lifestyle, we reevaluated our lives and felt like God was calling us to do something more.

Mike and I met on a blind date in high school in 1975. Our marriage was strong; we believed Bacalar was to be our new home. I was a high-school English teacher; Mike was a plumber by trade, but we longed for more. For more than 10 months we had been praying for God to reveal His purpose in our lives. Our pastor, Randy Bailey, and our church endorsed our decision to work with an independent, nonprofit missionary group called Missions International that our church supported and to become a part of something bigger than ourselves—to proclaim Christ to hundreds of unwanted children in this Mexican region.

Sharing the faith we had in Christ was important to all three of us. When I was 14, I gave my life to Christ while I attended a Christian revival in Houston. I vowed to read the Bible and learn all I could about Him. Mike had been reared in the Church of Christ, but his family at some point stopped attending. After we married, I pled with Mike that our own family needed to be involved in church. Ultimately we both began to desire a deeper relationship with the Lord and were hungry for the Word. We began attending the Metro Family Church (now Four Corners Church) in Plano. The Lord began to transform us. At age 13 Brittany made the decision to give her life to Christ. The three Terrells were excited about this new project of spreading the Good News in a foreign land.

Mike was to serve as the superintendent overseeing the construction of the clinic. I eventually would be the principal of the school. Visiting the region and serving as workers on volunteer teams for weeks at a time during recent summers only helped solidify our decision even more. We loved the area, we loved the people, and we loved the vision of Missions International, which had the goal of establishing churches, orphanages, medical clinics, homes, and to hold evangelistic crusades among unreached people groups in Central and South America, Africa, and Southeast Asia. On the volunteer trips we were energized to see the Mayans' eyes light up when we nourished their appetites and ministered to their souls. A sensation of new life ran through my bones; an humble nature and blind faith fed my spirit. This was an absolute dream-come-true for our family.

Everything went extremely smoothly with the sale of our house in Dallas. We knew God's hand orchestrated all of it. An estate sale of most of our worldly possessions netted us almost $9,000. This would go a long way in supporting our family on the mission field.

Raising support for our venture was extremely rewarding. Soon we were set to leave for our almost 3,000-mile adventure. We drove from Dallas to Bacalar in a truck with a trailer holding mission supplies and a few possessions for our family.

Bob Mason, the president of Missions International, fascinated us with his sincere love for God. To travel the world and spread the gospel captivated his entire family. God healed his wife, Debbie, of cancer in 1985. Subsequently, Bob became passionate about serving the Lord. Filled with the Holy Spirit, Bob and his wife began changing people's lives, healing the sick in Jesus's name, and taking part in the Great Commission!

Wow! Mike and I wanted to be a part of this whole experience. Both of us were so honored that we, too, would be serving the Lord. The fast-track to success and money in our prosperous North Dallas community had lost its luster; an unshakable yearning to fulfill God's plan replaced it.

One must learn to be still in this type of environment, an environment with essentially nowhere to go, nothing to do, and no one with whom to talk. The word *remote* didn't even come close to describing Bacalar. We soon learned to be content with our meager surroundings. In fact, we didn't even miss the TV too much!

Ninfa and José lived on the land that would one day house the orphanage. They were Mayan, descended from the great

Mayan Indian culture that dominated that region of Mexico from the time before Christ to the Spanish invasion. The Mayans are separate people from the Spanish and have their own language. They are small yet strong; Ninfa was no exception. Ninfa's slight stature fooled most everyone. She stood only four-feet tall, but she was strong as an ox and could cook up an incredible meal with very few provisions.

Black hair shot through with silver fell down her back to below her waist. A torn, old housedress covered her naked body; she lacked bra and panties. Her husband, José, often wore stained and torn khaki pants secured to his waist by a tattered piece of rope. A sundry of shirts or housedresses could be worn, but each possessed numerous holes and stains. The clothes the precious couple wore might have been aged and ready for the rag bin, but they were clean and appreciated hand-me-downs. The job of Ninfa and José was to ensure that no one stole any of the building materials. This they did faithfully.

The contrast between the lives of José and Ninfa and the lives of my friends in Plano, TX, were vastly different. While the precious husband and wife were content with their meager surroundings, in Plano, the race to acquire a nicer car, a more opulent house, and beautiful clothes seemed to consume everyone. In spite of their poverty, Ninfa and José smiled often. They never knew life might have more to it than mere survival.

Their house was made of black tarpaper and scrap pieces of wood with a *palapa*-style roof made of palm-frond branches. It was enclosed on three sides. Inside were two beds with wooden slats that served as their mattresses. The tarpaper walls were lined with shelves made from bamboo. In the front entryway was an open fire pit made of cinder blocks. A large, wok-style bowl stood where Ninfa prepared all of her meals. A faded, tattered, orange curtain served as the door. A large bucket served as the toilet. Soft dirt made up the floor and was quite comfortable except during thunderstorms when the powdery earth turned into a soggy muck. A generator ran the water pump and their little television. The dear couple had little else. But they were happy nonetheless. Every morning each of them would greet us with a smile that exposed rotten teeth. Even though they had but precious few possessions, José and Ninfa were content with what they did have.

Our days started early and were full of menial labor. The first several weeks were extremely rewarding with few problems. We usually arrived at the clinic site at around 7 a.m. We spent the cool morning, as it was only about 92 degrees compared to the more than 100 degrees it would reach by afternoon, digging, shoveling, mixing mortar, and a variety of other tasks around the clinic.

Our first task was to help the Mayan men finish the second story of the clinic. The labor was difficult. Sweat became our new best friend. Learning to mix concrete by hand can be quite a chore. The men, who were minuscule creatures, would carry concrete up a rickety, manmade ladder while they balanced buckets on their heads. Endless trips up and down the tiny ladder were necessary to accomplish even the slightest headway. The buckets must have weighed at least 50 pounds each, but I never saw one of the workers drop a single one. One might say what we observed was a circus act in the making!

Within one week we had two deliveries of cinder blocks. With callused and bleeding hands we unloaded approximately 5,000 blocks. We did this one block at a time. Here we had no forklifts to do our work; tough manual labor was required.

At night my body would ache as I lay down waiting for sleep. As each day closed, the workers gathered their belongings and began their long treks home. Mike and I enjoyed lingering on the property, reflecting on the day's progress, and dreaming of our future here. Ridding oneself of worldly possessions frees the spirit to experience life on a different plane. Being so connected to the earth and so disconnected from the material world was intoxicating.

Before I became a missionary, my diligent work and dedication to my teaching job simply served to secure material possessions for my family and me. I had fallen into the trap of trying to "keep up with the Joneses." Shopping on Saturday afternoons exhilarated me.

Now my focus and priorities shifted. Oddly, as I settled into Bacalar, I didn't miss the old life—not even one little bit. I was waiting in His vineyard and waiting for His plan to unfold in its entirety. Truly all things do become new in Christ Jesus! Second Corinthians 5:7 promises that "if any man be in Christ, he is new creature: old things are passed away; behold all things are become a new." I was becoming someone new. I whispered so many times, "Thank you, Father for making me NEW! Amen." I liked the new me.

The new clinic was situated about eight miles outside of Bacalar and only four miles from a military checkpoint, where the Mexican Army ornamentally displayed machine guns. The stucco structure proudly stood just off the highway purposely so that when finished, people could access the clinic. To help maintain security, a sloping, steep berm ran parallel to the highway and across the front of the property.

José and I spent numerous hours baking in the hot sun as we planted thousands of grass sprigs and fledgling tree sprouts that would eventually grow into beautiful, emerald vegetation. Hundreds of trees had been cleared by hand to ensure ample room for a circular entrance, which would allow room for ambulances and parking. The main road, which would meander throughout the entire property, proudly bore the name Jonathan's Way after the son of Andy and Heidi, the missionary couple that served before our arrival. The road would wind all the way to the lake over a mile through the property. Jungle, trees, and brush had to be cleared.

When one looked at the whole project, it seemed like an impossible task, but a believer knows that "I can do all things through Christ who strengthens me" (Phil. 4:13). The honeymoon stage of our assignment lasted about four weeks. Our spirits stirred with fulfillment and great anticipation as we waited for the Lord to unfold His plan.

Chapter 2

A Place in the Jungle

A cadre of missionaries served with us. Mike, Brittany, and I lived in a house on the lake, about 12 miles from the building site. Mike's peaceful nature and willing heart made his physically demanding job here a perfect fit for him. Growing up an athlete and loving sports in general, Mike had been able to dodge even a trace of the pudgy belly that plagues other 43-year-olds.

Our daughter, Brittany, was quite the beauty, with her translucent white skin and iridescent hazel eyes. Even though she was only 15, she stood 5-feet-8-inches tall. Beautiful, thick chestnut hair fell down to the middle of her back. Her smile would light up any room; she had a heart of gold. Her beauty surpassed that of any young woman I knew.

Mike and I couldn't help be aware that Brittany's fair complexion and shapely figure sometimes brought about unwanted, lustful stares by men with yearning eyes. Being loving parents, we wanted to protect her from these men's eyes and lustful thoughts, but locking her in her room wasn't an option.

Another person in our group was Brandon. He traveled to Bacalar with us from our church. He'd turned 18 and possessed no real desire to go to college. He decided he wanted to see the world, starting with Mexico. Wanting to find himself, Brandon asked to join us for three months while he learned a new language and experienced an unfamiliar culture. Brandon spent his days walking around town and saying *buenos días* to every person he passed. Visiting townspeople who enjoyed smoking marijuana while they watched the sunset was part of his secret weekly agenda. "Can I go explore for a while?" is how he would get out of the house. Brandon: just another person who kept secrets from us.

Daniel, a young man of 24, was a recent graduate from seminary. He longed to live without worldly possessions and to hear God speak to him. He had several months of time to donate before he was to begin working with a small church in Arkansas. Daniel possessed a unique gift of working with troubled teens. His own desire to rely on the Holy Spirit for guidance became the catalyst for his moving to Mexico and living with us.

Lastly was Bob, the president of Missions International, who visited us once or twice a month to work with the teams. Even though he didn't live with us full-time, he occupied the best room in the house when he arrived. Mike and I gave it to him out of respect. At six-feet tall he possessed a commanding presence. Peppery dark hair curled around his face and accentuated his steel-blue eyes.

This was our new family and support system. We worked together. We prayed together. We ate together. We learned to rely on each other and became each other's family. Each brought his or her own special gifts and talents to the group.

Volunteer teams flew into Cancun and traveled to Bacalar on a bi-weekly basis to help work on the clinic. Each team would consist of approximately 20 members and traveled from a variety of locations in the United States. Every group would bring people with an assortment of talents. One set might bring two or three electricians or carpenters, while another set might bring several plumbers, as they were in short supply but badly needed. The numerous bathrooms in the clinic were in dire need of attention. Thankfully, Mike was a gifted plumber and managed to do much of the work himself.

The remainder of the team would be ready to work dili-
gently as they toiled in the heat for four grueling days!
Workers would start the week proudly stating that they felt so
humbled to be helping with such a noble cause, but by week's
end, every member on the team would voice his thanks for
being blessed by the Mayans. These Mayans had nothing—no
cars, no heat during the winter, no fresh water, no dental care,
no surplus cash, but they were happy: happier than most of the
Americans who ironically wanted to save them.

Missions International acquired close to 600 acres of land
spanning from the main road all the way to the Lake of Seven
Colors. A jungle of vines, *chi chin* trees, and centuries of over-
growth hid the crystal blue lake from the well-traveled, two-
lane thoroughfare. Cheetahs ran wild throughout the property,
snakes slithered around through trees awaiting unsuspecting
prey, and killer ants contrived mounds reaching up to as much
as six-feet across and four-feet high.

Danger lurked in the stillness. Despite the tranquil beauty
of the vegetation, danger prowled in hiding. The *chi chin* trees
that peppered the acreage held a toxic sap that oozed from its
limbs with the swing of an axe. This sap could dissolve human
skin on contact. Once even the smallest drop of sap permeated
one's clothing or skin, it continued its black magic until blis-
ters begin to form under the skin and pus oozed and manifested into more sores.

A member of the Arkansas team, Allen, inadvertently took
one hard swing into a *chi chin* tree; he had mistaken it for
another type of tree. On impact, sap began to seep out of the
limb. Horror stuck his face as he freed his axe from the devil's
grip. Placing his hand on the tree limb for leverage, he realized
his fate. While he feverishly washed his hands, his skin began
to melt away. Pus began replacing the epidermis. By nightfall
chi chin sap found its way onto Allen's forearms, his right calf,

his groin, and into both eyes. Salve and clean gauze protected his vulnerable state from infection; bandages covered his swollen eyes; valium calmed his mind. Three weeks of a sterile environment and strong sedatives insured Allen's recovery with only minimal scarring to his eyes and forearm. Hidden within the darkness of the jungle, evil lurked around every tree and every bend. It took the form of a thick, oozing poison.

The darkness of the jungle hid danger from the Americans. The murky danger peered out from under Ancient Mayan ruins covered with creeping vines. Hidden within the brush and overgrown vines, dark eyes stared at us through the thick underbrush. A foreboding eeriness loomed around us as we walked through the property. We felt as if eyes we could not see were watching us, but they followed us nonetheless.

The property ultimately was to house a clinic which was situated by the two-lane highway, an orphanage made up of individual dwellings that would accommodate up to 90 boys and girls, a school, and assorted buildings for eating and worship. A huge *palapa* would sit proudly in the center of the property and would serve as a gathering place for worship, prayer, meetings, games, and the like. Each missionary family would have its own small house on the compound. Small, intimate structures in a variety of sizes were to serve as the homes for the orphans. Each dwelling would have eight to 10 children and a parent couple who would serve as the mom and dad. The philosophy of the orphanage was to model family units rather than housing the kids in one large dorm-like structure.

On some days Brittany and I did not go to the building site. While Brittany was excited about working in the clinic, where she would serve as the secretary, she did not relish the backbreaking task of the actual building process. While she was still in Texas, Brittany had had a vivid dream in which she was playing and singing with several small orphan children. The dream validated her purpose for giving up the good life back home. Even though she missed her friends in Texas, she, too, appeared excited about our new life.

Three days a week Brittany worked on her schoolwork (I was Homeschooling her while we were in Bacalar.) While she worked on her studies, I walked in the sweltering heat along the long, dusty road to the market. Now, that took some getting used to: no one to carry your groceries, many of which were freshly killed! Chickens still had their heads and feet attached and resided in a freezer, but the freezer wasn't plugged in! Getting to market early was important to avoid purchasing a spoiled chicken.

Most items could be bought in the market square, but the selection paled in comparison to any American grocery store. Even the small mom-and-pop stores in the United States house a variety of items, but not here. Brand names were nonexistent. Toilet paper felt like sandpaper but cost a small fortune. The lunch-meat selection consisted of ham or bologna. Our daily dinner diet changed from steak or pork chops to meager items such as pasta and *creama*, a Mexican condiment that goes on almost everything.

All shops closed for *siesta* from 2 to 4 p.m., except for the bread shop, which opened at 2 p.m. Milk was not from a cow nor was it kept in a refrigerator, since people didn't have any electricity, much less a fridge! Pigs and other carcasses hung outside of the doorways of meat markets, which hoped to entice customers. On many occasions the smell of the rancid meat in scorching heat made me want to vomit. This was not your local supermarket!

Learning to adapt to another culture takes time and patience. One must learn to understand and respect another's way of life. That was one thing we had plenty of—time.

After about two weeks of sweltering heat and backbreaking days, work on the clinic was wearing the teens pretty thin. Brittany, being the spokesperson, asked if she and the boys could walk around town in Bacalar and explore the shops. I thought, *No harm.*

"Sure," I said, "Be careful."

Thoughts such as *Where could they go?* and *Will she be safe?* lingered in my mind, but I remained silent. So off they went to walk around the town square. Shops and tiny restaurants encircled the plaza. Half of one street was filled with a double basketball court where Mexican males, young and old, played b'ball all hours of the night. In the center of the square a gazebo rested where young couples might cling to each other and dream of their tomorrows.

On this day, the kids were able to be American kids again. They ate hamburgers and French fries Mexican style. Brandon and Brittany walked into a piñata store, where crude creations of Goofy, Donald, and Klifford adorned the white stucco walls. The kids laughed at themselves as they stomped through puddles of water left from an afternoon rain shower. For a moment they were 5 again and enjoying innocent fun.

On Brittany's return she told about some precious puppies she had seen on the grounds of a restaurant. "Mom, they are so cute. Can we get one?" Brittany pleaded.

Just what we need, I thought but instead said, "We'll see."

A few days later Brittany and I found ourselves strolling around town. As we walked near the square, the sun peeked through fluffy white clouds. Brittany reminded me about the puppies she had seen a few days before. "Please, Mom, can we go see them?"

After a moment of hesitation, I said, "Sure, show me the puppies."

The restaurant, Club de Vela, where Brittany had seen the dogs, was situated on the outskirts of the plaza on the Lake of Seven Colors. Little did I know that this moment—the innocent act of entering this place to merely view some puppies—would change my life and my daughter's life forever. Little did I know that it would be the beginning of hell on earth—a hell that would seem to never end.

As we walked on the property, we saw chirping birds fly through the air. Soft, green grass felt like a cool carpet under my feet and led all the way to the crystalline sand. The beautiful sand outlined the area next to the aquamarine water. Peaceful *palapa*-style huts sat in the sand and welcomed tourists. A breeze rolled over the crystal water; rays of sunshine danced off the lapping waves. Music played from an outside bar, where several locals were enjoying a *cerveza*. This was not your typical American restaurant; a variety of animals resided on the premises.

In the far south corner of the property, a deer lived in a large, manmade, chain-link area. Two stout, white rabbits with gray floppy ears ate raw carrots in their cage. Several dozen yellow parakeets chirped a sweet song. Iguanas and exotic birds stalked the premises.

Off on the other side, lying in the sand in a large cardboard box, were three puppies suckling their mother. Brittany picked up the tan male runt. We were reveling in puppy kisses as a man quietly entered from behind us and introduced himself.

"Buenos días, me llamo Aldo, y éste es mi restaurante."

As I turned around to look at the man, I saw his eyes suddenly become riveted on my 15-year-old daughter. I didn't know much Spanish, but I knew enough to know he just said, "Hello, my name is Aldo, and this is my restaurant." His eyes quickly diverted to me, but the uneasy feeling remained.

Brittany and I communicated with him the best we could, but our efforts were mediocre at best. This stranger knew absolutely no English, yet he seemed very intent on making conversation with us. Boy, trying to speak with such a limited vocabulary was difficult.

He did manage to convey that the puppies were $100 each (US)—more than I was going to spend on a dog (and a lot more than many nationals there make in two months.) Puzzled as to why this man, who spoke no English, would be trying so determinedly to communicate with us left questions in my spirit.

Who is he? I thought and with a tinge of disgust wondered, *Why does he seem to be leering at Brittany?* I did not know whether he had seen Brittany before when she had visited on the property and seen the puppies for the first time, but a queasy feeling arose from the inside and filled my body. Brittany and I walked down the dusty and littered lane toward home.

I could feel the man's dark eyes following us.

Chapter 3

Miracles in the Midst of Trouble

One could never pull off an undertaking like our clinic-
orphanage enterprise in Mexico without knowing someone on
the inside. That person was Ayaella. Ayaella traveled in two
circles: with Christians who were honorable and with a tradi-
tion that runs deep with deception, payoff, and half-truths.
Ayaella had an extremely dark complexion and jet-black hair.
His khakis and crisp shirt appeared to be new and were always
pressed, an unusual site in the region. He spoke both English
and Spanish extremely well. Bob had worked side by side with
Ayaella in securing the property for the clinic and orphanage.
Clandestine meetings took place in which hundreds of dollars
would change hands between Bob and Ayaella for supplies and
the like.

I didn't know what the money was for and today can only
begin to speculate. Quite a bit of red tape needed to be taken
care of before all 600 acres could be deeded to Americans.
Some type of problem always seemed to be brewing just under
the surface. Mike and I were never privy to these inside dis-
cussions. I did draw my own conclusions: corruption and payoffs.

In the months leading up to our arrival, the *Junta* (social
services of Mexico) issued several deadlines for proper paperwork. But those deadlines were always extended after a meeting between the *Junta*, Ayaella, and Bob. Mike and I had visited the *Junta* ourselves on several different occasions, but we
didn't have the money or connections necessary to pull off this

project alone. Things in Mexico, especially things that have to do with the governmental branches, move at a turtle's pace.

Now, as I reflect on this project with a great deal more objectivity than I once possessed, I realize the task was a little too daunting for so few people. This project was to be built in stages over the course of several years. Doctors, nurses, and dentists had committed to moving down from various areas of the United States as different stages were completed. Quite a few members of the medical staff had already bought acreage on the lake and were designing their houses.

A missions organization, however, cannot run without money! Bob Mason had several projects going throughout Latin America and Cuba. He tried to devote labor and money to Bacalar, but doing so was difficult at times. With all of the many tasks that needed attention, a lack of funds and great need always seemed to exist. Mike and I never worried too much about fronting money for supplies. We would simply have Bob reimburse us. Perhaps that, too, was part of our naïveté.

On November 4, 2000, the project shut down. All Americans were ordered to stay off the property. We risked being thrown into Mexican prison for disobeying this order. We drove out to the clinic, where we were met with a guard standing out front and a huge chain and padlock, which made entering the land impossible. Tears wailed up in our eyes; our hopes began to fade. *Maybe we weren't meant to be here after all.*

A phone call to Bob was in order. He did not appear to be as shocked as we were. We knew that the process of getting the land's title had encountered some kinks, but we never imagined it would ever turn to this.

"Please, Mike, I need you guys to stay down there," Bob began. "I will be down in a week or so. I will get all of this straightened out. I promise. Besides, we have a team arriving in a few weeks. We need you there to take care of them," he added. "We need your help in building the new church in Limones," he pleaded.

Bob can be very convincing. We stayed.

Now our days were filled with nothingness. In our previous lives, we were busy with work, family, and church. We were great at juggling our hectic schedules to make room for everything and everybody. Now what? I knew that God was working on teaching me to be still, but not this still! Brittany, like the other young people, became especially bored and eager for something to pass the time. We filled our days doing little for God and more for ourselves. Driving to Chetumal, the next largest town, for lunch, window-shopping, and the like became the norm. Idle hands (and hearts) truly are the devil's workshop. Several times within one week we found ourselves at Aldo's restaurant in Bacalar.

One beautiful afternoon we decided to go to Club de Vela for dinner. A languid breeze blew off the water. Mike and Brittany were cutting up. All three of us were laughing and enjoying ourselves.

Aldo approached our table as we ate our meal consisting of grilled shrimp with onions, rice and beans with fresh tortillas, and *pica* (hot) sauce.

"*Buenos días*," he began. "How are you?" he asked in Spanish. Our Spanish lessons were paying off. In just a few weeks, Brittany and I knew enough of the language to communicate with Aldo, even if we did so on a very elementary level. We felt proud of our improvement.

Aldo complimented our progress in learning Spanish so quickly. I knew Spanish on a superficial level, since I had taken it for 11 years while I grew up in Houston. Likewise, Brittany knew some of the language because she took Spanish in the sixth and seventh grades. She also had several Hispanic friends who aided her in becoming familiar with the language. Poor Mike was another matter. He knew no Spanish and was quickly finding out that he did not have an aptitude to pick it up either.

Aldo stood at the table and told us us that his daughter planned to arrive from Argentina at the end of the week. "She speaks English," he said proudly while he exposed his ill-kept teeth, a common sight in this region because of the lack of nutrition and dental care. "I'm sure she'll want to meet you," he added. I still sensed that he looked at Brittany with desire in his eyes. I felt my old uneasiness return.

Needless to say, Brittany became ecstatic at the news about Alejandra's arrival since our daughter did not have one female friend with whom she could communicate. She missed her friends desperately, so maybe this would turn out to be a blessing in disguise. As I watched my daughter's eyes light up with wild excitement, I began to wonder whether Alejandra's presence would make Brittany more content with her surroundings. In turn this would make all of our lives a little easier, or so we thought.

We were not that familiar with the Mexican culture, but we were impressed with the fact that Aldo had been so affable. He was a small man about 45-years old. He had dark chestnut hair, an umber complexion, and shadowy, almond-shaped eyes. Despite his awkward appearance, he appeared to be genuinely pleasant. Moreover, he seemed interested in our project. He even offered his assistance if needed. He lived above the restaurant with his wife, Yamelle, and her two children.

We were beginning to think that we could wait for the clinic to resume. The long and lonely days were spent trying to befriend some of the Mexican people and educate them as to the purpose of our mission. Bacalar as a whole was not thrilled at the thought of white people arriving in the community trying to change their way of life with such luxuries as medicine for the poor and dental care for all.

Brittany and I began looking for something of value to fill our days. We sought out opportunities to help some of the residents in the area. We soon learned of an orphanage in Chetumal where young children were cared for. The children ranged in age from 6-months to 8-years old. After gaining clearance, we began to volunteer at the orphanage several days a week. Many of these young boys and girls were born with birth defects or mental retardation. Others were merely abandoned on the side of the road. Many of the parents had no way of caring for them, so each was placed in the orphanage to be looked after.

One little girl, Isabella, was brought to the orphanage because of malnutrition. While her mother and father fed themselves until they were obese, they starved little Isabella. They left her on the stoop of a neighborhood church. She was 3-years old and weighed 24 pounds. Each time Brittany walked into the ward, Isabella's eyes would light up like a Christmas tree as she held out her emaciated, pencil-thin arms. Once Brittany picked up the small child, letting go was next to impossible. Isabella would mumble and cry to be held just a little longer. She was starving for more than food. She needed human companionship.

Isabella lived almost four weeks before she died in her sleep. Her body had been stripped of all love and nourishment. Her little heart gave up; it stopped beating during her peaceful slumber. Seeing such cruelty and lack of respect for life broke our hearts. Brittany and I continued to visit the orphanage, but doing so became increasingly emotionally difficult as the weeks passed. Day after day these dear children lay in their beds, often tied to the bars so as not to crawl out, waiting for the pain to end and perhaps to be lucky enough to die in their sleep as Isabella had.

Miracles can happen even in the remote village of Bacalar. The people in the community knew that we were missionaries. Besides, we stuck out like sore thumbs! On previous occasions several local natives in the area had visited us to ask for food, money, or clothing. Helping others was our purpose; we felt great in doing so.

One day in mid-November, a woman arrived at our gate and asked whether I would go with her and pray for her husband. I walked with her to her small house, where she introduced me to her husband, Manuel. As I walked up the dirt trail, I noticed his unkempt appearance. His hair was matted from both sweat and dirt. As I drew closer, I looked into his eyes. I saw pain. Before words were spoken, his eyes drew me into his world of poverty and ill health. Manuel's knee was swollen. Pus oozed from cracked scabs in which gangrene had begun to fester.

"Pray for him, madam, please," the sweet woman said in Spanish.

Oh, my gosh, I thought, *What can I do for him?* I was definitely in need of a real miracle here! We were waiting for our own divine intervention in dealing with the clinic. I wasn't sure my spirit was filled enough to help someone else.

But I decided to obey the Lord and pray for this precious man with pleading eyes. He and his wife expected a miracle! They had the blind faith of children unscarred by cynicism. As I took a deep breath, I knelt beside the man and began stroking his swollen leg. My heart trembled as I began, "Father, please heal this poor man's leg. Clear the infection from his knee. Make him whole in Christ." I laid my hands over his fevered knee. With my eyes closed, I felt the Holy Sprit with me. I was not alone. I continued to pray for the infected knee and hoped that a miracle would happen. Full of the Holy Spirit, I walked home and thanked God for the opportunity to represent Him in such an awesome way.

A few days later I drove by their house to see how Manuel was doing. He was sitting on the front porch. As I walked up to the house, Manuel's eyes met mine. He had a big a smile. He walked toward the truck.

Wait, I thought. *He's walking!* I looked down at his leg; it was healed.

Manuel began speaking rapidly in Spanish about his miracle. God healed him!

Wow! I thought. I had been a part of a real miracle. I felt dizzy with joy. "Thank You, Father," I shouted. *"Glori a Dios! Glory to God!"* I whispered as I reveled in this amazing sight. Just days before, this man was praying that the doctor wouldn't have to cut off his leg to keep the gangrene from spreading.

I was so humbled that God would use me to work a miracle for Him! A pastor once said, "We do what we can, and He'll do the rest." God includes us in the working of miracles. I gave what little I had. I was blessed beyond measure at the Lord's faithful hand.

"Incredible!" I exclaimed as I walked back to the truck. *Maybe we were meant to be here after all.*

Chapter 4

A Way In

Alejandra's arrival called for a Mexican celebration at the restaurant. We felt a bit odd, as we were the only ones at the fiesta besides the immediate family. Aldo beamed with joy with his daughter on his arm. At 24, she was a beautiful girl, although one could hardly help noticing that Alejandra wore a revealing top made of light blue, gauzy fabric and tight jeans that showed off her curvaceous figure. Long, dark tresses fell down to her small waist.

In spite of the girls' age difference, Brittany and Alejandra melded like sisters. Alejandra, like most Latino people, was in dire need of dental care. She was extremely striking until she opened her mouth and exposed a set of extremely crooked and crowded teeth. The entire evening she clung to her father. Each stared at the other with an unusual gleam of longing in their eyes. They seemed to be more than father and daughter, but perhaps it was my own unfamiliarity with the Latino culture and its reverence of family. I hoped that's all it was.

On a regular basis Aldo's silver tongue enticed us for lunch or dinner. Increasingly often we found ourselves visiting the restaurant, where we dined with Aldo and Alejandra. Not wanting Brittany to intrude on a daily basis, I usually went with her and sat in the sun while she spent hours listening to music and bonding with Alejandra.

In the days of mid-November, we spent even more time with Aldo and his daughter. With Alejandra translating, we would while away the days sitting in the warm sun or discussing Mexican or American politics or a variety of other topics. Discussing matters with someone from another country seemed quite interesting, especially since we had little else to do. We were beginning to consider Aldo a true friend.

One day while we enjoyed lunch, Aldo questioned me about why I thought Brittany's finishing high school and going to college was important. This seemed to be a strange question; after all, an education had been good enough for his daughter. She had recently graduated from college. Many kids in this area complete only up to the 8th grade. Then they help out with the other children at home or work in the family business.

"In America," I began. "Children go to school until the 12th grade. Then most go on to college. That's what we're planning for Brittany," I said.

"What if she doesn't want to go to college?" he questioned.

"Well," I began, "she has to finish high school first. Then we'll see about college."

"But she told me that she doesn't want to go to college," Aldo blurted out.

"That's weird," I said. "She's never said anything like that to me."

I darted my eyes toward Brittany. She looked a little smug. We argued for a few minutes about who knew what was best for Brittany. *Pretty strange!* Puzzled by this conversation, I couldn't overlook his questioning and authoritative tone. Later, his words haunted me. I couldn't dismiss his challenge to my parental authority. I wondered how he knew so much about my daughter's secret dreams and desires.

We were bored and restless. Days turned into weeks. After Bob promised to visit with the *Junta*, we had no further word from him. No teams arrived because no work was to be done. Mike and I had absolutely no idea what to do.

Mike had been in steady contact with Pastor Randy about the clinic. After Pastor visited with the elders of our church, we received an email from him. Money had been raised for our return to Texas for Christmas. Boy, a break was in order. Hooray, this was wonderful news! The whole gang was excited. Getting to see everyone would be great! I missed my friends terribly. We were all starving for McDonald's hamburgers and French fries and real American food. The three of us fantasized where we wanted to eat first. We would have a race to see who could eat the most food. All of us were eager to be back in Plano again, even for just a few weeks.

The week before Thanksgiving, Brittany walked into my room and lay down on the bed next to me. A soft, gentle breeze off the lake made the room comfortable in spite of the heat. I laid my Bible, which I had been reading, on the bed and said, "Yeah, Brit. What's up?"

"Hey, Mom," she began, "Let's go somewhere for the weekend. It would be fun to get away for a few days. I'm so bored. There's nothing to do. Let's go somewhere so we can buy authentic Latino Christmas presents for everyone this year."

"Hey, Brittany," I said, "That sounds like a great idea. Let me talk to your dad and see what he thinks." A change of scenery would be a welcomed change.

It was decided. We would make our own adventure by exploring Mexico.

Merida, our destination, is one of oldest and most beautiful cities in all of Mexico. The weekend was nearing; our family was excited about a new quest.

On Thursday afternoon Brittany made a request. "Dad," she began, (we were always in trouble when she went to her dad first) "can Alejandra go with us on the trip? Pleaseeeee, can she go with us?" Brittany begged.

"Well," Mike said, "I don't know; let me think about it."

When one of us ever said, "Let me think about it," it meant, "YES" to Brittany.

Mike and I talked things over and saw no reason why Alejandra couldn't accompany us. By Friday afternoon the four of us were off to Merida for an exciting weekend.

Cobblestone streets filled the city. Horses' hooves clopped along the streets with carriages brimming with tourists. Old mission churches and other governmental buildings lined the main thoroughfare. On our arrival, we noticed a festival. Colorful costumes of bright orange and blue filled the street. A joyful atmosphere lingered in the air. Even while we ate, we could hear the mariachi music playing in the distance. Vendors selling their wares made a circle around a beautiful marble fountain. Walking around the square, we inspected each vendor's wares. The goods were so different from anything one could find in the United States. After much consideration, we purchased a Mexican manger scene for my parents, a traditional poncho that displayed all the colors of the rainbow for my brother-in-law, a small but beautifully carved mahogany box for our son, Chris, and a turquoise necklace for me.

The weekend flew by; the time arrived to return home. "Wow, this was so much fun," I said. "We'll have to do this again." We had a great time and immediately began planning our next excursion.

Thanksgiving was fast approaching; we were in search of a turkey. Because we were Americans looking for a turkey to observe an American holiday, the gobbling bird was worth more. The locals wanted 400 *pesos* for a turkey! No way were we going to pay that much. These were the same birds that walked in and out of houses in my own neighborhood. After an extensive search through the rural area, I decided, "We'll just have hens."

Bacalar housed about 25 Americans. We knew quite a few of them. They all longed to celebrate a traditional Thanksgiving minus the football games and parades.

As Thursday approached, we finalized the menu for 18 people. Each person would bring something that he enjoyed in years past. The challenge manifested itself in finding just the right ingredients for the traditional recipes. Most of us had to be very inventive in trying to make our individual dish turn out as close as possible to the real thing.

After a huge meal, we played cards and swam in the lake—not even close to traditional activities for a Thanksgiving afternoon in the U.S. The evening sun was setting; the day had been fruitful. We were making new friends and learning new traditions. Each American living in Bacalar had a unique story as to how he or she ended up in this remote region of Mexico. Mike and I said our goodbyes to Brandon and Daniel, as they were both returning to the States.

After our new friends left and the sun began to set, Mike and I sat on the back porch that overlooked the beautiful, sparkling water. We reflected on how good we felt being away from our materialistic past.

"Mike," I began, "are you happy here?"

Mike looked out over the aquamarine water as it turned to a silvery azure and said, "Yes." He let his answer sink in. A beautiful silence filled the air before he began again, "I know it sounds odd, but I am happy."

A peaceful easiness filled the air—one that we had not felt in quite a while. Being here with only a few meager possessions felt freeing. The spirit seemed to be able to rest and be content.

"Today was a good day," I added as I leaned into him. We lingered on the back porch for a long while.

Aldo and Alejandra had not been able to attend our Thanksgiving celebration. Instead on the following Saturday they invited us to their restaurant for an outdoor cookout. When we arrived, Aldo was grilling onions, peppers, pork, and chicken. The grill contained enough food for 20 people, but we were the only ones invited. The aroma of roasting onions filled the air.

Over the stereo speakers, a male sang a beautiful Spanish song. Aldo proudly stated, "That's me! I sing, too!"

Mike and I looked at each other in amazement. *Wow*, I thought. *He owns a restaurant and sings.* We were amazed at Aldo's many talents.

During dinner Aldo once again turned the conversation to Brittany. He began, "Have you ever thought about Brittany becoming a model?" His eyes always seemed to turn to a dark stare when he looked at my daughter.

I was shocked. *Where'd that come from?* I thought as I wrinkled my brow. Brittany was beautiful, but I never thought of her as having a model's figure, so I said, "No, not really."

"Well," he began again. "I have. I think she would make a wonderful model in Mexico." He attempted to wait for the shock in Mike's face to disappear, but began again, "She has light skin and dark hair. She could be famous. I think she has the perfect look," he said with a crooked smile.

I looked over at Mike and saw that he was as dumbstruck as I was. But Aldo was not deterred and continued his outlandish proposition. "Would it be all right if I hired a photographer to take some pictures of Brittany? You never know. An agency in Mexico City might just see potential," he said very convincingly.

Mike and I wished he would drop the subject. But he continued, "I'll set up a shoot and take some pictures; then I'll send them to a contact in Mexico City. I still keep in touch with a few people from my performing days. "

Dazed and a lot confused, Mike and I did not know what to say. Our faces revealed the horror in our spirits.

Brittany, on the other hand, was quite flattered and begged her dad to let her try. "Please Mom, please Dad, let me do this," she pleaded, "Let me try, please."

"Let's talk about it, Brittany," Mike said as he leered at Aldo for even mentioning the idea in the first place.

The devil had just slithered into our weakest link: Brittany's desire for validation.

"What harm can it do?" I asked Mike once we were home and able to talk freely.

"I don't know, Vanda. Something just doesn't feel right about all of this. Where did this idea come from? I'm sure he's going to want something from us in return!" he continued. Those words would be long remembered.

"Mike, this is every girl's fantasy—to be a model. I think we should let her do it," I said, again with naïveté.

Mike's wisdom lost out to Brittany's wanderlust for approval. I, too, was swept away by Aldo's magical words.

The modeling shoot was scheduled for the following Thursday at the restaurant. A makeup artist and hairstylist transformed Brittany into a beautiful woman.

"She's wearing too much makeup!" exclaimed Mike. "It makes her look too old. I don't like it," he protested.

The photographer assured us that the extra makeup was necessary for the camera. Brittany posed on the dock, by the *palapa* bar, and lying in the sand. The shoot lasted several hours. Then the hoopla was over for the day. The photographer said the proofs would be ready in about a week.

Brittany couldn't wait. She just knew this was going to be her big chance.

Mike and I regretted this day. We would for years to come.

The next week was extremely busy as we finalized our plans to return to Texas. With the help of our pastor and church friends, plane tickets were bought in Chetumal. Special Christmas gifts purchased in Merida were wrapped in shiny, red paper.

The few winter clothes we owned were pulled from our powder-blue storage bins and packed. Soon we were on our way to Belize to the airport.

Filled with excitement, we felt that the plane ride took only moments. "Welcome to Dallas-Fort Worth," the captain of the plane said over the intercom as we flew over Big D. The Terrells had landed.

Eager to see us, our family and friends greeted us at the gate with hugs, flowers, and kisses. Being home felt wonderful.

The two weeks in Plano felt like three or four days. We had so many people to see, so much to do, and so many places to eat. We took turns staying with family and friends. Most of our days were spent eating out at some of our favorite restaurants.

One of our main concerns had to be addressed with our pastor. With the clinic closed and no immediate hope of it reopening, we needed to discuss whether returning to Bacalar was a good idea. Pastor Randy had visited with Bob on the phone. Bob reassured Pastor Randy that everything would be up and running soon. After several hours of discussion, we decided that our family would return for one month. If the clinic did not reopen, then we would move back to Texas.

On our return to Bacalar, we found a note on our front door from Alejandra. It read:

Please come over as soon as you get home.
I miss you. I have a present for you!
Come quick!

Love,
Alejandra.

She did indeed have a Christmas present for Brittany. Likewise, we had bought Alejandra a sweater. Brittany's spirit stirred with excitement to exchange gifts with her new friend. Reluctantly we drove to the restaurant as darkness set in over the lake.

As things turned out, Aldo and not Alejandra was the one who had a gift for Brittany. In fact, he had a very expensive gold necklace with a medallion. Mike and I wondered if we wanted her to keep it.

"Please, Daddy, it's so beautiful, and it's from both of them," Brittany pleaded.

"It's fine. There was a big discount on the necklace," Aldo said in Spanish as he looked at Brittany.

Mike shook his head and said, "OK, whatever!" She kept the necklace.

Another mistake.

A few days passed before we went to see the proofs from the modeling shoot. Much to our surprise, they turned out great. With the smile of a Cheshire cat, Aldo encouraged us to send several of the shots to talent scouts in Mexico City.

"Well," Mike said, "I guess so. What could it hurt?"

"Aldo," Mike continued. "How much do we owe you for the pictures?" he asked.

"No, no!" Aldo exclaimed. "It's my treat. I'm glad they turned out so well," he continued in Spanish with a smile that exposed his discolored teeth.

"OK," Mike said. "But if you hear anything from a modeling agency, we want to pay for that."

"*Buenos!*" Aldo said.

Brittany and Aldo were filled with excitement, but Mike and I were apprehensive about the desired outcome: Brittany's fame. After seeing the photos and Brittany's grownup figure, Mike and I wished we could erase the modeling shoot. Her beauty was only enhanced by the makeup and the professional hairstylist's magic touch.

The devil has a sneaky way of moving into your life and allowing you to consent to things you would otherwise never consider. The first week of January, Aldo asked if Brittany could accompany Alejandra to the doctor in Chetumal.

"The girls can have lunch and go shopping. They can make a day of it. Please, I need someone to go with Alejandra. I don't like the idea of her going by herself," Aldo pleaded.

Mike and I agreed, but our spirits were filled with uncertainties. Aldo assured us everything would be fine.

"Mike, I'm sure we're worrying for nothing. It'll be fine," I said.

Famous last words. All would never be fine again.

Chapter 5

In Trouble's Grip

January 6, 2001. We had not seen Brittany all day. She and Alejandra had gone to Chetumal for their planned day of shopping, lunch, and a doctor's appointment. Filled with excitement at the opportunity to go somewhere by themselves, they guaranteed us they could be trusted. During the past few months we had taken the 30-mile trip with Alejandra, but this was the first time they had gone without a guardian.

Brittany had spent the night with Alejandra so they could get an early start. Mexican women, for the most part, do not drive; therefore, Aldo's driver, Ernesto, drove the girls into the city early that morning and then would return later that afternoon to pick them up at the square.

Chetumal is the capital of the state of Quintana Roo and is a relatively large town. Dirty city streets are filled with shops and vendors awaiting Mexican and European tourists. This area is extremely popular for those who enjoy Mayan ruins, many of which are still pristine and not commercialized.

Brittany's newfound freedom felt awkward for Mike and me, so we wanted to make sure that we discussed the parameters backward and forward.

"I got it, Mom. Everything will be fine. I promise." Brittany said.

Aldo had assured us that his driver was trustworthy and that all would be well.

After Alejandra's visit to the doctor, the girls were to eat lunch at a local favorite restaurant that made the best *cerviche* and *tortas* anywhere. After feasting on handmade delicacies, they would pass the day window-shopping. The girls knew that they were to be home by 6 p.m. and that Brittany was to be dropped off at our house.

8 p.m. Then 9 p.m. Mike and I grew worried that something might have happened to Brittany and Alejandra.

They should have been home before now.

With each passing minute I grew more anxious. Questioning my own judgment and myself, I said, "Where is she? Why has she not called?"

Looking at Mike, I begged, "Please, go see if you can find out anything."

We had to know if Aldo knew where the girls were. As Mike pulled out of the drive, I had a knot in my stomach.

Approaching the restaurant, Mike noticed that an eerie darkness loomed over the property. The full moon cast strange shadows that caused men passing by to become distorted figures lurking in the night.

As Mike exited his truck, his heart began to beat with anticipation. A large Mexican man approached him. "Can I help you?" the man asked in Spanish.

Mike tried to communicate that he was looking for Brittany and Alejandra. Without a word and with a blank stare, the man turned around and walked into the inky darkness.

Not knowing much Spanish or anyone in town, Mike decided to head home. His heart pounded; his body shook as he drove. "Where could she be?" he wondered.

His mind reeled with unanswered questions as he drove down the dark lane.

I heard Mike wheel into the driveway. As he entered, his face spoke what words could not say. "They're all gone. No one is there."

As he stared at me, he could not speak further. His face was pallid. Words could not convey the expression on his face. With tears in his eyes he finally whispered, "Where is my girl?"

Overcome with disbelief, I tried to search my mind for a hint of where she could be. "Did she say they made other plans?" I asked aloud.

Nothing made sense; we were fearful that something horrific happened. Every parent's nightmare was unfolding before our eyes: our daughter was missing. We had no clue as to her whereabouts. Our hearts grew heavy with dread and fear.

With little to go on except the trepidation that filled our bodies, we went upstairs and proceeded to lie down to sleep. The night was still. Water slapped against the dock in a rocking motion. On most evenings, this sound lulled us to sleep as the fan sliced through the thick, warm air, but on this night sleep eluded both of us. We lay in bed listening to the uncanny silence. The hours ticked by.

Waiting for sleep to rescue my mind, I began to recall a precious memory about our daughter. It was Father's Day, 1998. Brittany had been practicing endlessly for a special presentation for Mike. After a wonderful barbecue and swim at Mike's sister's house, Brittany asked everyone to sit down. She had a special gift for her daddy. She put on music cued to Bob Carlisle's song, "Butterfly Kisses."

The music began; Brittany appeared from the hallway. Dressed in her bathing suit and a pair of white butterfly wings, she rhythmically moved with the music and matched each phrase from the song with a gesture. The room lay silent. We sat mesmerized by her fluid movements. She appeared to float through the air.

As the song ended, she fluttered her hands and sat in her father's lap. "I love you, Dad. Happy Father's Day," she said.

This was such a precious moment. "Butterfly Kisses" belonged to Brittany and her dad.

Through the years, Mike often sang along to the song on the radio as we ran errands. On many occasions, as I glanced at his silhouette, his eyes would fill with tears as he mouthed the words to the song. The dance only made the song more cherished. Brittany was truly Daddy's girl. As the memory began to fade, my heart ached to see her eyes as she looked on her dad with such love and adoration. Somewhere, reveling in the sweet memory, I drifted off to sleep.

As the sun began to appear over the lake, we rose at 5:15 a.m. and began worrying all over again. During the morning a spirit of restlessness began to envelop me. As I paced around the house, I had a sickening feeling that Brittany was in danger. I could not shake it. The feeling only intensified with each passing moment. So I decided to go see Rosie.

Rosie and her family had become like kin to us. We thought of her as much more than just our Spanish teacher. Their home and land has been in Rosie's family for more than seven generations. The pink stucco exterior had been tortured over time by sun, torrential rains, dogs, and a multitude of children. The glass in the windows had long been removed; bars were installed for security purposes over the openings.

As I pulled up in the truck, her children ran out the door and beamed with bright smiles as they called my name.

"*Señora Vanda, tienes dulces para mí?*" they cried with sweet, innocent laughter. They were accustomed to my bringing them candy or a special treat. I did not smile nor run to catch them. I did not have a treat for them today.

Rosie stood in the doorway. She must have sensed my apprehensive demeanor. She walked me around the side of the dwelling into the unkempt side yard where her mother, Rosita, washed clothes and the children played ball in the cool evenings.

"Rosie, Brittany is missing." I whispered as I walked under the damp clothes hanging on the line. "She did not come home last night. The restaurant is deserted." I began to cry as I spoke those words. I closed my eyes and hoped I would wake up from some horrible dream. At that moment it hit me; *something was terribly wrong.*

"Rosie, will you go with me to the restaurant?" I asked. "Will you please help me speak with Yamelle? Maybe she will be able to tell us something."

As we climbed into the truck, I saw Rosie's face. She was trying to be her cheerful self, but I saw her young eyes fill with worry.

During our previous visits to Aldo's restaurant, we had learned more about Yamelle. She actually was Aldo's common-law wife. He had been living with her for the past seven years. They had met while Yamelle worked at a local gentlemen's club in Chetumal. Yamelle served drinks and danced in the club.

Animal attraction overcame Aldo, for Yamelle was a sensuous Latino woman, with chestnut hair and a curvaceous body. Yamelle most likely noticed Aldo's bankroll. She already had two children when she met Aldo.

They had a peculiar relationship that perhaps only people of the Mexican culture can appreciate. Yamelle kept her own apartment in the city and often stayed in Chetumal for days at a time. Her children were often farmed out to various family members. She and Aldo did not have a typical marriage according to American standards.

The restaurant was deserted. The *palapas* were empty: no tourists sunned themselves on the sand, no waiters walked around in uniform. A dead silence replaced the usual Latino beat of the Mexican music. Aldo was gone. Alejandra was gone. Boxes were piled up all around the outside of the premises. Yamelle's whereabouts were unknown. No one knew where Aldo and his daughter were, or at least, no one was telling us.

We also had learned that even though Aldo pretended to own the restaurant, he was simply the manager. We decided to visit the Superior Beer factory in Chetumal, as it owned the eatery. While we talked with the owner, we discovered Aldo recently took 30,000 pesos from Superior Beer as an advance. "He was planning on changing the menu and needed extra cash for lobster and other shellfish," the owner said.

We seemed to be not the only victims of Aldo's silvery tongue. This information only heightened our fears and left us with more questions—questions no one was willing to answer. The owner of Superior Beer put out an "official request" for Aldo to return the money within 72 hours, or a warrant would be issued for his arrest.

Driving home, Rosie suggested we go back to the restaurant and inquire again as to Yamelle's whereabouts. "Perhaps she will be there and we'll have better luck. After all, we do have some new information," she said. "Maybe she honestly doesn't know where Aldo is either."

"Rosie, do you really think she'll talk with us?" I asked. "I know I'd be mad if my husband left me without so much as a 'howdy do'!" I said with doubt.

I stared out the window to drown out reality even if only for a moment. I gazed at small, half-broken *palapas* with holes in the roofs. I wondered if people actually lived in the wretched hovels. My mind was tired of thinking; my body was numb, so I peered through the window at naked children playing with sticks along the highway, women balancing large baskets of papayas on their heads, and mangy dogs wandering the dusty road. Mike drove the long, winding path back to Bacalar. The sun was setting. A cool breeze moved off the lake as we pulled into the restaurant once again. A whole day had passed. We knew nothing.

When we arrived, Yamelle was working behind the bar. Workers filled the sandy beach once again as they cleaned and prepared the *palapas* that peppered the property. With our hearts pounding, we walked up toward the bar, where bugs swarmed around the single light illuminating Yamelle. As we approached Yamelle, Rosie began to speak to her in Spanish. Yamelle answered quickly with a sense of urgency and anger.

Gosh, I thought, *I wish my Spanish was better!* Yamelle began to yell at Rosie. Then she blurted out some words in English.

With contempt in her voice, she spoke in English for the first time. "You stupid Americans. Alejandra is not Aldo's daughter; she's his friend! He sent for her. She came all the way from Argentina to be here with him."

At that instant, I felt a hot knife sear through my stomach. I felt as if I had been kicked in the gut. I could barely stand, but I forced myself to listen as Yamelle continued, "Aldo, Brittany, and Alejandra have left Bacalar. They are not coming back."

I reeled in disbelief. My eyes widened as my body began to go numb. "This couldn't be happening to us," I thought. There has to be another explanation. He's 45-years old! Why her? What could a 45-year-old man possibly want with my 15-year-old daughter?" I asked with such naïveté.

I looked at Mike. Horror filled his eyes. My mind reeled at the possibilities. We had little to go on and nothing concrete to take to the *policia*. But trying to put the pieces together by ourselves was driving us insane.

We attempted to let the shock wear off as we took Rosie home. Alone, in the dead silence, Mike glanced at me. We knew we had to make the dreaded phone calls to our family. The song "My Redeemer Lives" played softly.

"What do we tell them?" I whispered.

"I don't know," Mike said as a single tear fell down his cheek.

How do you prepare for such a phone call? "Hello, Mom, Dad . . . Brittany is missing. We don't know where she is, who she's with, what she's doing, or . . . IF SHE'S ALIVE!" What do you say at a time like this?

Mike and I each called our parents, our pastor, and then we made the most difficult call of all. We called our son, Chris.

Chris was seven years Brittany's senior and lived in Jackson, WY, where he worked as a carpenter helping build high-end log homes. Brittany's protective older brother had never wanted us to take Brittany to Mexico in the first place. Now we were calling to tell him that she was gone.

"Dad, I knew something like this was going to happen," our son responded anxiously. "It's Mexico, she's only 15, and you shouldn't be taking a teen-ager to a foreign country. She should be in a normal high school, for God's sake. What happened? Where do you think she is? Do you want me to fly down there?"

Mike said, "Slow down, Chris," as he tried to answer each question.

I could hear only Mike's side of the conversation, but I could tell Chris was devastated. My body was shaking all over. I paced from the den to the kitchen and back again. I couldn't

54

sit down. My heart thumped loudly. I felt as if my chest would explode any minute. Mike attempted to answer Chris's questions as quickly as they were fired off, but this was difficult because Mike, too, found himself in a hazy fog. The facts were crystal clear. Brittany had been gone for two days. We hadn't heard a word.

Then it was my turn to speak to my firstborn. "Chris, hey son," I said softly. My eyes began to well up with tears as I listen to his words of assurance.

"Mom," he said in a soft voice, "it's going to be OK. She'll call you. I'm sure she has some kind of logical explanation." Chris's voice was full of love and kindness. All of the angst he felt while talking with his dad dissipated as we began to talk.

I couldn't imagine the shock he was going through. My two children had been close. "OK, son," I said quietly. "I'll let you go. We'll stay in touch."

Tears streamed down my face. I wanted to hold Chris and have him hold me. His voice felt like velvet. It was so soothing. I wanted to pull him through the phone and throw my weary arms around his broad chest. The desire of a mother's heart is to be close to one of her children when the other is in danger.

Mike looked at me and walked toward me. I buried my head into his chest. "We'll find her, I promise," he proclaimed. "We won't leave Mexico until we do."

Exhaustion overtook our weak and frail bodies as we climbed the stairs. We both longed and wished for sleep to invade our souls and over take our weary minds. That night we lay in each other's arms and wept while we prayed in desperation.

"Please, God let us find her." "Oh, Father, we trust You, but we are dying. Help us find find her, Father."

After many moments of silence, Mike softly began to speak. "Vanda," he began. "God did not give us a spirit of fear, but a spirit of power, of love (2 Tim. 7). We can't let fear take over our spirits."

I began to release the tension throughout my body. "Yeah, you're right," I said as he held me close. "Fear is of the devil. He lurks in darkness. Be gone in Jesus' name."

As we lay in bed, with each of us trying to comfort the other, we listened to the droning fan slice the hot air. We wept softly. After many minutes, sleep slipped over us like a mist over the lake beneath us. Our minds would rest, even if for only a few hours.

Chapter 6

Grasping for Answers

The answering machine was blinking when we walked in the front door. Someone had called; we had missed it. Mike and I had visited our favorite local restaurant for breakfast. I usually looked forward to eating *huevos rancheros* for breakfast at the Mexican Café. But I didn't this morning. Today I had mashed my eggs and beans together and made an awful mess.

Scurrying as fast as I could, I pushed the "play" button on the machine.

"Hello, Mom. It's Brittany." My heart surged.

"Thank You, God," I whispered. He had answered our prayers. If only we hadn't left, we could have spoken to her. How could we have been so stupid to leave the house?

The message continued, "I'm fine. We're in Cancun. We're going to stay with Aldo's cousin."

WHAT? I thought. *Here we are going out of our minds, and she's on holiday!*

The message continued, "Aldo is going to sing at the Ritz Carlton on Friday and Saturday. Then we'll be coming home. I'm sorry we tricked you. I love you. Please don't be mad!"

"Don't be mad!" I screamed as I flailed my arms in the air. "What does she think she's doing? Who does she think she is?" I had never tasted anger such as this before. My whole body was shaking with scorn. I closed my eyes. Tears began to flow as I sank to the floor. I felt so betrayed: betrayed by Brittany and by Aldo.

"How could Aldo let Brittany sneak away without asking?" I wondered. Mike stood staring at the machine as though the mere act might cause Brittany to materialize out of thin air.

We listen to the message again. "Mike, what does he think he's doing? How would he feel if we took his daughter without asking?" I questioned.

Mike shook his head, but he remained motionless. We listen again and again and again. Something didn't sound right. She sounded too happy.

"Mike," I said, "she doesn't sound like herself." We listened to the tape again. My mind couldn't wrap itself around the changes in her voice. "What could this evil man have done to her already?" I questioned.

Then, thinking quickly, Mike called information and got the phone number for the Ritz Carlton Hotel in Cancun. He called and spoke to the clerk at the front desk.

"OK," he said, "so you don't have an Aldo singing this weekend? What? You've never heard of him?" he said slowly as he turned to face me. "OK," he said as his lowered his head in despair.

Mike placed the receiver back on the cradle, looked at me, and said, "Vanda, no one has heard of him. They are not there."

He swallowed hard and with a look of lost desperation asked, "What are we going to do? Here we are in a foreign country, can't speak the language, and WHAT ARE WE GOING TO DO?" He screamed.

Mike's calm demeanor had been replaced with rage, hurt, hatred,and fear.

My heart felt as if it had cracked in two. Betrayal, anger, hurt, and despair enveloped my soul. We needed a REAL MIRACLE—NOW! With doubts filling our spirits and nowhere to turn, we called out to God in desperation, "HELP

US!" I didn't feel too holy at this moment, but we had nowhere to turn. So, in our darkest hour we turned to Him. Fear crept back into my spirit.

"Mike," I said. "I'm so afraid something has happened to her. We might not ever see her again."

At that moment he reminded me of the Scripture in Romans 8. It states "God did not give us a spirit of fear that makes [us] slaves to fear." We were seasoned Christians. We knew heartache. We knew better than to succumb to fear. But nonetheless, it overwhelmed us. We were both paralyzed by it and called out to God.

We fell to our knees. We cried out to Him, "Abba Father, please help us." Amidst the tears and prayers of desperation, we felt His spirit begin to comfort us. As a Christian, I knew to lean on Him in all things, but at times like these, we become so human, so dysfunctional, and so arrogant.

As we hung onto each other, we sensed our angst begin to subside. Our spirits calmed. We felt Him say, "Lean on Me."

Broken and crushed, I cried, "Oh, God, why? Why is this happening to us?"

Mike and I held each other for a long while. Then Mike whispered, "Vanda, I think we need to go to the police."

"Yeah, I think so, too," I said with my head lying on his shoulder. We sat in each other's arms on the floor as we tried to gather our thoughts. We wondered whether we could go on.

Confused and weary, we made our way to the police station but not before picking up Rosie so she could translate for us.

"Lord," I said with a small voice and a grateful heart, "thank You for Rosie. Without her I don't know what we would do!"

We pulled up to the small, dilapidated, filthy building lined with a variety of Mexican men. With its harsh rays the sun baked the dry earth. Wild birds walked around the yard and picked through garbage strewn all over the ground.

As we exited the truck, I noticed a frightening group of Latino men sitting on the front stoop. Standing alone, away from the crowd, one man leaned against a skinny tree and cupped his left hand under where his right elbow should have been. He wore a bloody gauze bandage that appeared to be rounded at the end where the blood pooled into the dressing. The night before his arm had been cut off above the elbow with a machete. He waited in the scorching sun to file a complaint against his friend. The man had been part of a group of drunk Mexicans arguing over who had the hottest woman.

The Mexican culture believes that males are close to being gods themselves and believe in the idea of male superiority known to the Latino culture as *machismo*. Evidently one of the men got out his machete and chopped the guy's arm off.

"Ouch, that's gotta' hurt." Mike said as we eyed the man. Mike held me close as to protect me from some evil force that seemed to permeate the province.

Questioning as to whether visiting the police station had been a good idea, I said, "Are we sure we want to go in there? We might not come out." Mike and I were extremely nervous about even walking into the station, but Rosie insisted.

Memories from movies about Mexican prisons invaded my mind as we reluctantly made our way inside.

The muddy, grease-smeared walls of the station were lined with handmade, worn, wooden benches that were covered with stains that had obviously come from a variety of bodily orifices.

"Oh, how horrible," I said in disbelief as we walked inside of the station house. The pungent smell of sweat and urine filled my nose as we scanned the room for a clean place to sit. We didn't find one.

I thought to myself, *Never in my wildest nightmare would I ever have imagined being here waiting outside a Mexican jail to tell authorities that my daughter had been taken by a 45-year-old acquaintance who last week I would have called my friend.*

The three of us sat scrunched in the cleanest corner we could find. An unused mop stood up against one wall. In the opposite corner, crusted vomit pooled on the floor. Dirt lingered in the air. This place was not for the faint at heart. Again, I wondered, *What are we doing here?* But I remained silent and trembled quietly.

A small, elderly Mexican man motioned us to the back of the station, where he led us down a long, dark hallway into a small, poorly lit office. The tiny hallway had no ventilation. It felt at least 120 degrees.

A middle-aged man sat behind an old, rickety desk. He picked up a soaked rag and began to wipe the sweat from his brow. "Have a seat," he said in Spanish. "How may I help you?" he asked. Rosie had to translate everything for us. This slowed down the process. Rosie aided us in telling the captain our story.

The officer was acquainted with Aldo and told us his name was not Aldo but rather Abel Martine Lopez Rodriguez. He added that he was not Mexican but from Argentina.

The captain did corroborate the fact that Alejandra indeed was Aldo's daughter.

I closed my eyes and shook my head slowly at the sheer disbelief of the whole situation.

As I said before, no one in Bacalar has secrets except from the Anglos. It seemed as if the whole town knew a deep, dark secret but forgot to tell us!

The captain appeared to be genuinely interested in our plight. The police were helpful and their attitude assuaged our fears just a little. Interested in finding out where Aldo and

Alejandra might have taken Brittany, the captain listened intently to our story. Several other policemen overheard our conversation from outside the doorway and mentioned to the captain that maybe they should go to Cancun and check out the story one way or another. The police felt that Aldo, Alejandra, and Brittany might still be in Cancun even if Aldo wasn't singing at the Ritz Carlton. We didn't have any leads in Bacalar. We were going crazy with worry. Maybe this would pan out.

Three police officers, Rosie, her youngest baby, Mike, and I piled into a small police vehicle and began the four-hour ride to Cancun. *Uncomfortable* could never describe how miserable we all were in the car. In the heat of the day, it can be 112 degrees. With no air-conditioning, the ride was laborious; without knowledge of Brittany's whereabouts, the ride was excruciating.

This two-lane road was peppered with grave markers to show where Mexicans both young and old were run over every day. This thin road bared no shoulder on which people could walk or ride their bikes. Dense brush and lush vegetation encroached on the road in places. Many large trucks must travel this slender, two-lane road to deliver goods to many remote *pueblitos* and villages. For many, it is a road to death—a death that lurks from behind, where at least they do not see the death angel as he strikes his unsuspecting victims.

Markers and small marble vaults where candles burn lined the roadside by the hundreds. Young boys are remembered: they sold pineapples on the roadside for one *peso* (10 cents). Fathers traveled on their bikes into the next town: to work as a *valador* for 10 *pesos* a day ($1) to provide food for their families This road connected the superstitious, voodoo-practicing jungle to the aquamarine paradise of the Mayan Riviera. We had taken this trip more than a dozen times to pick up teams at the airport in Cancun, but until this particular day I had not noticed the rancid smell of decay.

Rosie's cousin lived in Cancun. We were going to stay with her family for a few days, or at least that's what we thought.

Ultimately we stayed three long weeks in Cancun as we looked for Brittany. We looked in some of the most horrid places: numerous strip joints, houses of prostitution, and places that sell young girls.

Chapter 7

The Daunting Search Begins

On arriving at Lupita's house, we were greeted with hugs and were able to take warm showers. Christmas had been the last time I had showered with hot water. The scalding water at Lupita's doused my body. I wanted to remain in this safe, warm haven indefinitely. My senses blocked out everything except the warm refuge of the shower. But soon I heard a slight knock at the bathroom door. Rosie whispered, "Vanda, you need to hurry. It's Mike's turn. Lupita and her husband, José, were extremely kind to take us in on such short notice." In my stupor I was being careless to endanger the house's warm water supply.

After we cleaned up, we went to the police station. The police station in Cancun was larger and cleaner than the one in Bacalar, but it held the same bureaucracy. Everything in Mexico—especially the police—moved very slowly. The Bacalar police filled in the Cancun police on the story. One of the top police officers began, "Let me ask around. I am sorry about all of this. But I may be able to help you. I have some connections with many people—some who are involved in drugs and prostitution. I have to keep myself informed on what's going on, you know. Let's also check out the Ritz Carlton thing just to be sure that Aldo's not performing there."

Mike and I were pleased, as the man seemed to be really on top of things. Finally, a glimmer of hope appeared. "Thank You, God. Please let something come of this," I said as we drove through the streets of Cancun listening to Aaron

Jefferies sing on CD, "I Go to the Rock." We sang along to the song and for the first time in several days felt optimistic.

We went back to Lupita's house, where she had dinner waiting for us. Lupita fixed a wonderful Mayan *sopa* with fresh cilantro, chicken, and a variety of vegetables served over white rice with fresh flour tortillas. Mike ate because he was anxious and restless and I, once again, played with my food for the same reasons.

Internet is an enigma in Mexico. Many cities have Internet cafés, where one goes to email friends and use the web. In Bacalar we had all set up our own accounts through Yahoo mail. The Internet café was just down the street from Lupita's house. Mike and I thought we might email Brittany. *Maybe, just maybe she would be able to email us,* we thought.

"OK, what do we say to her?" I asked. Mike began typing. "Brittany, are you OK? Do you know who Aldo really is? What do you know about Alejandra? You are in danger," we wrote. "Please email us if you can. WE ARE LOOKING FOR YOU!!!!! WE LOVE YOU. WE WILL FIND YOU."

We will find you. Somewhere, out of the recesses of my mind, I recalled the words . . . *We will find you.* I had heard this vow before. My heart began to pummel the inside of my chest as Mike typed the email. Then, just like it was yesterday, I remembered. One night while we had dinner with Aldo, he asked me, "Vanda, if anything every happened to Brittany, what would you do?" He had looked at me with challenging eyes that spoke of defiance.

"Oh, my gosh. Mike," I began with horror in my eyes, "do you remember that night when Aldo asked me what I would do if anything ever happened to Brittany? Do you? Mike, I told him that I WOULD LOOK FOR HER FOREVER." Quivering all over, I almost dropped to the grimy floor. Aldo had challenged me to the greatest of all duels. He took our daughter right from under our noses while he pretended to be our friend. And he even used his own daughter to do it. What kind of man does that to his own daughter? "Mike, he planned this all along."

Leaving the Internet café, Mike and I feared that we would never see Brittany again. Mike looked at me with sad eyes. "She has to write us back. She just has to. Please, Brittany, email us so we know you're OK," he cried out. At least six times a day during the next week, we checked the Internet café but found no response.

Mike, Rosie, and I (in better circumstances, we might have been the Three Musketeers) visited the police station every morning. The first three days we were all very hopeful that we would find Brittany. Every morning at 9 a.m., we arrived at the main station and waited for news. Often we waited up to an hour before we saw an officer. We had learned the ways of the culture. You must wait. Eventually an agent would walk outside the building and update us on what was accomplished the previous day, but not until he was good and ready. We saw no use in trying to hurry the situation along; in fact, it only prolonged the agony.

On day two the officer said, "Last night we followed up on a lead. We think that she might be involved in a group who sells young teens," he said. He looked very important behind his dark, mahogany desk. "If you could give us some money, we will visit a local contact and see if he can find anything out for you," he continued.

Paying the police off is nothing new. After all, they were trying to help us, so we shouldn't mind helping them. They weren't after much money, but they always had their hands out. Bribes and payoffs: if they would help us get Brittany back, we didn't mind. We would arrive at the police station with high expectations and leave disheartened and discouraged.

Everywhere we turned, people asked us what she looked like. So we decided to make some posters of Brittany, Aldo, and Alejandra. At Kinko's we made hundreds of MISSING posters with Brittany's picture on them. "Have you seen my daughter?" I would ask with tears in my eyes while I held up a picture of Brittany's beautiful face. I looked at the faces of strange Mexican people as they nodded their heads NO, but their eyes reflected despair only a parent could know—a despair that crosses all language barriers.

I tried not to get discouraged, but some of the places we went in this big city scared me. Many of the old buildings in the downtown section of Cancun are disguised as hotels but are in fact brothels. A tourist would not be able to tell the difference between an actual hotel and a brothel, as both have a front desk, tourist pamphlets, and a clerk. The only difference: in one location you get a room and a girl!

We had pictures of Aldo and Alejandra to pass out on every street corner. After several days of passing out flyers and receiving only bad news, the Bacalar police officers decided they needed to return home. Mike and I feared that Brittany might call home again. *What would happen if we were not there?* With an overwhelming fear of missing her call, we decided that Mike would ride home with the Bacalar police, forward the phone to Lupita's phone number, and drive back to Cancun in his red Dodge pickup. Besides, we needed a vehicle if we were going to continue our search.

So Mike made the four-hour trip back to Bacalar, packed some clothes, drove four hours back to Cancun, and arrived back at Lupita's at 3 a.m. He had barely fallen asleep before he needed to rise again. As the bright morning sun began to peek over the horizon, Mike and I didn't know if we could even go on another day. We never knew what the new day might bring: promise or despair.

Scared and anxiously awaiting Mike's return, I walked around the neighborhood for hours. I had to wait all day before Mike would return from Bacalar. "OK," I thought, "I'll go check my email again."

Click. *Wait, I have mail from Brittany!* My face grew flushed; my heart thumped. I felt as though my heart would pound out of my chest as I pressed the *open* button, click.

Dear mom & dad:

You wrong bout Aldo. He nice.
I don't know why you say such mean things bout Aldo.
Don't look for me.

The message continued with broken English. I reread it again and again. *Words are inverted. Words are missing. Surely my literate daughter did not write this message.* I printed off a copy and took it back for Rosie to read. Maybe she could solve the riddle. I raced back to Lupita's house and showed Rosie the email. She read it and then read it again.

"Vanda, I don't think Brittany wrote this. She speaks perfect English. Someone else wrote this email, or someone told Brittany exactly what to say."

With this news, fear encroached on me. Someone was controlling Brittany's every move. I waited for Mike's return. More questions began to permeate my brain, but I had no answers.

Anxious, I lay awake in bed. I stared at the ceiling fan and listened to the grating squeak as the blades glimmered in the darkness.

When Mike arrived at 3 a.m., we read the email together. More questions were raised; we felt more concern as to her whereabouts and her safety. Again, no answers.

On the sixth day the police told us that perhaps we might try looking at the strip joints on the outskirts of town. Officer Rodriguez said a common practice was for men to take young girls, both Mexican and American, and place them in these strip clubs where they whore the girls out. Just when I thought that it couldn't get any worse, it did!

"We are getting nowhere coming here to the police station every day and hearing nothing," Mike said. "I'm going crazy just sitting and waiting. I want to do something to try and find her myself." He told the policeman, "I am willing to go to these clubs every night if that's what it takes."

"But you need someone to go with you who speaks Spanish and who can arrest Aldo if we spot him," the officer said.

"Arrest him?" Mike said. "I'm going to kill him."

I knew he spoke only from anger and fear. He really wouldn't kill Aldo. *Or would he?*

Officer Rodriguez agreed to go to the clubs with Mike. Nightfall arrived. Several police in plain clothes arrived at the house, where we talked about Aldo, Alejandra, and Brittany. The men had in their possession pictures of all three so they would know what each one looked like.

When the hour struck midnight, Mike and the police loaded into the truck. Off they went to the girlie clubs. "The Devil's Lair", or the prostitution strip, lies about 15 miles outside of Cancun. Few tourists know about this side of Cancun's splendor.

The first club they went to was called All Girls, All the Time. It advertised young American girls. In the men went.

Smoke curled through the bar. Latino music blared through the speakers. As they walked through the place, girls strolled around with bare shoulders and partially exposed breasts. Almost no clothing draped their frail bodies. The men took a table in the back so they could watch the front door, the stage, and the back door. They sat down and ordered a few drinks.

Mike began pulling out his pictures. One of the cops said, "Hang on. Let's wait and see if we see one of them." After about an hour, they began canvassing the premises and showing Brittany's picture to several men. With wanton desire, dozens of men ogled Brittany's physique. They may not have seen her, but from their reaction to the photo, they sure would like to meet her. Heads shook. "No," the team heard over and over.

Just as they were starting to get discouraged, Mike heard, "I've seen her." Mike glanced at an overweight, dark man about 50-years old. He wore freshly starched black jeans, a crisp white shirt, and a straw cowboy hat. Mike walked over to him and showed him the picture again.

"Are you sure?" Mike asked.

"Yeah, I've seen her. She's strippin', but not here. She's at the Total Nude American Girls club down the street."

"Are you sure?" Mike said.

"*Sí*," he said. "She's only been around for a week or so. But I don't think she's dancing this late. Her man has her workin' the streets after 2 a.m."

Through his horror, Mike showed him a picture of Aldo. "Yes, *sí*, that's him." Mike's spirit was breaking at this news, but he thought, *IT COULD BE WORSE!* Mike and the officers decided that because the hour was late, they would go to Total Nude American Girls the next night. They drove home.

Mike's head hung low with desperation. Mike pondered quietly as to how he was going to break the latest news to me.

Seven days had passed. We had one email that we were not even sure was written by Brittany. I had not slept nor eaten more than three or four bites at each meal. We were beginning to realize that she could be anywhere in Mexico by now. I had been waiting on pins and needles since midnight, as I hoped against hope that the phone would ring or that Mike would return home with some news.

Not knowing was eating away at me. I tried to remain calm and not become panicked. The hours ticked by like thick, brown molasses. I heard the crackling asphalt as Mike's truck pulled up to the house.

The front door opened. Mike could hardly get it shut before I bombarded him with, "Well, what happened? Did you find them? Has anybody seen her?"

"Slow down, Vanda. I'll tell you. Hang on." He began, "Vanda, girls as young as 12 or 13 strip in these places. They are so thin and frail. I can't imagine any of them wanting to be there."

Tears streamed down my face as he told me about the young girls. "Vanda, men gawk at these adolescent girls. Their worn, dirty hands caress the girls' most private places and kiss their young bodies all over. It's sickening to see these lustful men ogle over these precious young bodies. The girls stare with blank looks. They no longer reside in their own bodies," Mike murmured as he sat next to me on the sofa.

"This could be Brittany's fate. Think about it, Vanda. These girls belong to someone. They have parents who are just like us: scared and frightened for their daughters' safety." We had never known a horrible life such as this ever existed. It only continued to compound our own fears about Brittany's fate.

Clinging to each other for strength, Mike murmured, "Let's get some rest."

"I can't sleep, but OK," I replied. "Father, please let Brittany be safe tonight. Father, please let her have a safe place to sleep," I prayed in a pleading cry.

As we collapsed, broken and exhausted both physically and mentally, sleep enveloped us with its tender arms.

Chapter 8

Silver Lining

On the morning of January 17, 2001, I received a phone call from the local newspaper in Bacalar. Brittany had been missing for 11 days. The newspaper wanted to do a story on Brittany's disappearance. A reporter arrived at the house and asked us a million questions. We went over the details. As the reporter took the picture of Brittany from my trembling hand, she commented, "She's so young and beautiful."

"Thank you," I said softly as my fingers clung to the photo.

"The article will run tomorrow. If anyone calls with any type of lead, we'll let you know," the reporter stated after the interview.

Mike and I hoped that the news article would bring some fresh leads in the case. Once again we had a glimmer of hope; if only it would last.

The afternoon ticked by slowly. For hours I lay on the concrete patio in the front yard and let the Mexican sun beat down on my thinning legs and arms. The heat reminded me that I was alive. Someone had to stay home in case the phone rang, but hours went by in silence.

Mike and Rosie returned to the police station to check on leads. Everyone was preparing for a trip back to the strip clubs, where we hoped someone would spot Brittany.

We did find one silver lining in our dark cloud. It happened when Mike and the officers went off for another late-night search for some answers. They were working off the lead that they had been given the night before. Total Nude American Girls was the first stop.

As the heavy, wooden door swung open, the smell of cigarettes, stale beer, and cheap perfume filled the air. Mike dreaded going back into the devils' den, but he had no choice. The men walked in carefully so as not to draw attention to themselves. They again located a table that was strategically positioned where they could see most of the bar and dance area.

A grinding, slow cadence began to blare from the speakers as a young girl with dark hair strolled on stage. Her long legs were partially covered by black fishnet hose. The hose ended mid-thigh, where red garters secured them. Chestnut hair flowed over the girl's face as she rubbed her young body up and down a pole. The music enabled the girl to transport herself into a fantasyland where just she and the music existed.

As Mike watched in horror, he found himself wondering out loud, "Brittany?" It startled even himself. His heart almost stopped as he looked at the girl on stage.

He canvassed her body for a sign that it was his precious daughter. Mike couldn't get a good look at the girl's face as she was twirling her head around with the beat of the seductive music. *Wait,* he thought. *Brittany's taller. This girl's hair is longer.* His heart skipped a beat as he cried out, "Thank You, God!" Conflicting feelings of fear and relief flooded his mind simultaneously.

Something (probably the Holy Spirit's prompting) in his gut told him to talk to the girl, so Mike waited to visit with her after she finished dancing. Approaching her with caution, he sat next to her at a table. The young girl sipped a soda and appeared oblivious to Mike's presence.

He spoke softly, "Hello, my name is Mike. I was watching you dance a moment ago. What's your name?" he asked.

"Maria," she said.

"Maria, how old are you?" he inquired.

"Fourteen," Maria said with her head hung low.

"Where are you from?" Mike questioned.

"Limones," she said.

As they began to talk, the young girl opened up to Mike. She and a cousin had waited to take the bus from Limones to Felipe Carrillo Puerto to help out a sick family member. They lingered on the dusty, two-lane road that traveled from the outskirts of Bacalar to Cancun. Waiting in the hot sun for the bus and hoping it would arrive soon, the girls talked. Then, out of nowhere, an old, blue sedan careened off the road in a swirl of dust and offered them a ride. Before the girls could say no, two men got out of the car and forced them into the back seat. The girls had been brought to a small hovel just behind the dance club. A bodyguard kept a close eye on them at all times.

Mike was horrified. "How often does this happen?" he thought. Mike motioned for the officers to join him and Maria at the table. They began looking for Maria's cousin. Mike said to her in a gentle voice, "Don't worry. I'm going to get you out of here."

Mike learned that both girls were only 14-years old. They had been missing for two weeks. One of the girls looked very similar to Brittany, only her skin was slightly darker. The girls began to weep as Mike and the two officers carried them out of the strip club.

No one dared to stop them as they exited the club. "I think it's time to go home," Mike said as he helped them into the truck. The girls wept gently in the back seat as the men made the arduous trip back into the city.

Mike traveled to the police station with the girls to make sure they remained safe. Parents were called; tears of joy fell as the girls realized they were actually going home. Mike was grateful that his search at the club, although fruitless for our family, at least had brought joy to some other parents.

The time was 4:30 a.m. Mike decided to return to Lupita's house, where hopefully he could get some sleep.

Asleep on the couch, I awoke to hear the truck pull up to the front of the house. Mike entered the den with a saddened look of hopelessness. Again, he held me as he told me of the events of the evening. "Vanda, I am beginning to wonder if we will ever find her. There is so much evil in this world. The families of those two girls didn't have the money or the resources to find them," he whispered.

"Don't you know they were mourning quietly and wishing for a miracle just like we are?" he added. Tonight we dare not speak of Brittany's fate. We walked into the small bedroom and lay on the bed hoping against hope that she was still alive.

The next morning the newspaper arrived. The article was on page three. It included a picture of Brittany, a synopsis of her disappearance, and a plea of help from anyone who might have information as to her whereabouts.

Mike and I dressed and drove to the police station again. We were escorted into the captain's office. He informed us that the police could do nothing more. He explained that his men had already spent too many hours looking for our daughter. We were on our own. He added that if we found her, they would help us in any way they could.

We walked out of the station and did not look back. Another door closed. As we drove home, Mike turned to me and asked, "Now what?" We were losing hope fast. How many rejections were we going to be able to endure?

However, as one door closed, another door opened. A reporter from one of the local TV stations read the article and wanted to do an interview. We drove to the station immediately and were taken to a small interview room, where we met

Ernestina, a voluptuous, middle-aged woman of about 50. She wore a chocolate-brown suit with a tangerine-orange crepe shell. Her jet-black hair was pulled into a tight bun that accentuated her large, almond-shaped eyes.

"Hello," she said, "My name is Ernestina. I'll be doing the interview. But first, let me say I am so sorry for you. I can't imagine what you're going through. I have three girls of my own. I would die if something happened to one of them!" She continued, "We are going to do the interview outside. So if you will go outside and wait for me, the film crew is waiting." No sound checks or anything like that. Just a "Let's begin"; the camera began to roll.

Being a seasoned reporter, Ernestina looked into the camera and began telling the Mexican people about our plight. Within moments, the camera was on us. She asked us several questions. "Where are you from? What are you doing in Mexico? What happened to your daughter?"

And then looking at me she asked, "Do you have anything you would like to say to the Mexican people?"

With my heart pounding, I began, "I love your country and the people. Please help me find my daughter."

Tears began to flow from my eyes. *Would these people even care about some white Americans losing their daughter?* I wondered as I tried to remain calm. Refocusing on the task at hand, I went on. "Aldo," I said in a dejected voice, "if you have our daughter, please return her to us. We will not hurt you or press charges. Just bring her back to us safely."

I then looked into the camera and said with tears pooling in my eyes, "If you have seen my daughter, please help us!" At that moment, I was hoping against hope that someone had seen her, would feel our heartache, and would turn in Aldo.

Through the years I had watched as couples on TV pled for their child's life. Every time, my heart broke. But now, Mike and I were the ones pleading on TV for the safe return of our baby girl. We were begging some heartless man to return our dear child to us. It almost didn't seem real. This all seemed to be some gigantic nightmare from which I couldn't wake.

We thanked the camera crew and returned home to wait. I had never been good at waiting, but God's hand had gently instructed me. He helped me learn to quiet my spirit and to be still. Time can be such an enemy in situations like this when all one can do is wait.

Driving through the dusty street of Cancun, I reflected on the interview. I recalled saying, "I love your country and your people." I realized that I harbored no fear or hatred for the Mexican people as I once had. I truly loved the Mexican culture. My disgust for Aldo had nothing to do with his cultural heritage.

Evening arrived with no word. We saw the piece air on TV at least four times in late afternoon. Anxious and exhausted, Mike and I sat on the sofa and read our Bible. We turned to Isaiah 43 and let His words minister to our weary souls. Mike read, *Do not be afraid, for I am with you; I will bring your children from the ends of the earth.* The Scripture gave us a minute of peace.

I began to pray, "Father, please reveal someone who has seen her. Keep her safe until we can reach her. Thank You, most heavenly Father, for Your comfort. Amen." We closed our eyes and blocked out the world for a moment and found peace through His love.

As the sun began to set on another day, I decided to walk to the Internet store to check my email. "Maybe Brittany has had a chance to send us a message," I thought.

Wishful thinking. My account was empty; no messages received.

78

Entering the house, I heard Mike on the phone. He was talking to Brittany!

What? She called? I thought to myself. Adrenaline rushed through my body in the matter of a millisecond. *Wait, he's yelling at her! He's arguing with her,* I thought as I walked in the front door.

"NO, Brittany, we are not going to stop looking for you!" I heard Mike shout. He hung up the phone and looked at me with wild eyes filled with anger. "She says she's fine and for us to get that stuff off the TV, or she's never coming home!"

I squeezed my eyes tightly shut, "What?" I asked as I shook my head in sheer disbelief. How I wished this was only a dream!

"She said that she's not with Aldo and Alejandra and for us to stop looking for her!" he exclaimed.

Anger welled up inside as a lump formed in my throat. "We know she's not fine; we know that she's with Aldo," I said. "She's afraid of her own shadow. In fact, up until last year she could hardly go to the bathroom alone. Does she expect us to believe that she's wandering around a foreign country by herself?" I questioned loudly. "How stupid does she think we are?" I asked as I paced around the small den. "Aldo put her up to this," I continued raging. "He's the one who doesn't want his name blurted out all over Mexico."

Once again we were filled with anger, dejection, and a sinking feeling of despair that this would never end. The adrenaline rollercoaster was certainly taking its toll on my psyche.

I looked over at Rosie. She was so kind and gentle. Her large, almond eyes watered as she searched for something comforting to say.

"It's going to be OK. Let's have something to eat," she said as she tried to encourage us. I sat at the table and willed myself to eat, but doing so was impossible.

After dinner, we sat in the living room and stared at the walls for what seemed like hours. What was left for us to do? Every lead dried up like a dead leaf. Mike called our son, Chris, and updated him. They visited for a few minutes about Chris's job in Jackson. Chris was a free spirit. After recently graduating from Brevard College, he moved to Wyoming to enjoy nature's grandeur.

Chris is a natural athlete. His six-foot frame was lean. Chris has sandy blond hair and sparkling blue eyes. His smile captivates everyone—his incredible smile! He is an expert skier, mountain biker, and hiker. Chris and Brittany had a special bond despite their seven-year age difference. Brittany looked up to her big brother and almost worshiped the ground he walked on.

Concerned, he began, "Dad, do you want me to fly down there?" he asked. "I think I can find her," he added.

"No, Chris, I don't know what you could do that is not already being done," he said. "I'll call you when we find out anything."

Mike placed the receiver on the phone and looked at me with sad eyes. We sat in silence with nowhere to turn, no one to help us, and a daughter who said she didn't want to be found.

The phone rang again. It was Heidi, a friendly voice. Andy and Heidi had served as the missionary family in Bacalar the preceding year. We had worked in tandem during the transition period. They showed us the ropes. They, too, once had uprooted their family to move to this remote part of the world. They were well aware of what living in this country and working with its bureaucracy was like.

Andy and Heidi lived in Nederland, TX. One summer when they still resided in Texas, Heidi had gone to visit her parents in Missouri and left Andy in charge of the family.

Andy had thrown a little party for their son on his birthday. In the car on the way home from the party, Tanner wanted to have a bite of his birthday cake. He couldn't wait until they got home.

"Please, Daddy, I want some cake now," he whined. Andy pleaded with him to wait until they got home. The anxious young boy couldn't wait, took a large bite of the dry cake, and began to choke.

The choking intensified. Tanner was choking severely. Andy was yelling at him from the front seat, "Lift your arms!" "Breathe, son," he screamed. Before Andy could pull the truck over safely, Tanner began to turn blue.

Tanner died on the side of the road before the ambulance could get to him. Andy held his son's lifeless body in his arms. "GOD," he screamed, "NOOOOOO!" He sat on the shoulder of the road and wept bitterly. The accident was tragic. Only after many years and a real miracle did the couple begin to heal.

Now Heidi had called and reached out to me! "Vanda," Heidi began, "Please let us fly down and stand with you. Our church people want to help you out monetarily. They are sending us down to bless you. We want to be with you."

We were amazed by the fact that Andy and Heidi wanted to fly down and help us heal with companionship. They were flying in the next day from Dallas. My heart longed for emotional support from someone who knew heartbreak.

Mike and I met them at the airport. When Heidi's eyes met mine, I broke down. Seeing Heidi's beautiful face, I collapsed in her arms. I began to sob, partly because I was overwhelmed at the idea that they would travel all this way to stand with us, but mostly because they truly could share our pain.

Pain and loss are funny bedfellows. We think we know what pain and suffering are until we find ourselves in the midst of hell itself. Then we resent those who are content and happy. My weakened human spirit was beginning to show its vulnerability. Reacting gracefully when someone says "I know how you feel" is difficult.

I heard those well-meaning words at least 50 times a day. They made me want to shriek! I wanted to scream and ask the one speaking them, "Has your child been taken? Is your child missing? Well, then, NO, you don't know how I feel!" Heidi knew exactly how I felt.

But in my heart I knew that people are shocked and grasping for something to say. They are terrified for us and for themselves. After all, the roles could be reversed. Tragedy can befall anyone at any time. Friends and acquaintances can't imagine how we survived—how we managed.

"Oh, my, how do you do it?" they asked. "How do you go on?" they inquire.

"You just do."

Quite frankly, I have asked myself that very question at least a million times. I have no logical answer. Only by God's grace was it possible!

Rosie's warm smile greeted us as we pulled up to the curb with Heidi and Andy in tow. Rosie had been the Spanish teacher for this couple as well and felt a kinship for them both. Heidi and Rosie had lots of catching up to do since Heidi's family moved back to the United States. Pictures of Faith and Jonathan, Heidi's two surviving children, were shared. My, how fast children grow up!

As they sat on the couch, I reflected on just how lucky we were to have Rosie. She was a gift from God. Her family was poor. Her loved ones lived in a small house with only the bare necessities. Mike had thankfully been able to fix their shower that had been broken for months before our arrival. Rosie was only 25 but already had four children. For hours each day she worked preparing meals for her family and for two missionary boys who lived at their church. She did not share my faith because she was a Mormon. But she loved and cared for us nonetheless. Rosie sacrificed her time and energy for Mike and me. It was a debt we would never be able to repay.

Mike and Andy talked about the clinic's progress. They discussed possibilities about how to reopen the project. For the first time in the past several weeks the conversations seemed normal and light. Laughter and enthusiasm filled the air.

We all sat in the small den in Lupita's house and discussed everything we knew so far about Brittany's abduction, which turned out wasn't much. We stayed up most of the night talking, crying, and sharing. We had been in Cancun for three weeks. In many ways it felt like a moment; in others it felt like a lifetime.

Andy mentioned that he knew a lawyer in Bacalar who was well-connected in the region and might have some contacts. Besides, Rosie needed to get back home to her other three children, her husband, and her other responsibilities (other than babysitting us). For too long we had kept her from her family and job. Returning to Bacalar sounded like a good idea.

The background surrounding Andy and Heidi's move back to the States from our project had remained a mystery for more than two years. Secrets surrounding this whole project remained steeped in deception.

As we began to learn now from Andy and Heidi, the story was far more complicated than we could have ever imagined. Before they left, Andy attempted to pay out of his own pocket the union workers who worked at the clinic site because Bob had said he was low on money. Andy didn't have enough money; many bills were not paid.

The union bosses became enraged. The union in Mexico is connected to the mob! Subsequently, the mob put out a contract on Andy's life. Through his connections, Andy found out about this and decided that he was not willing for his family to sustain another loss. They left—in a hurry! We were never privy to any of this information and therefore had no clue what was going on. As we were arriving to help out with the project, Andy and Heidi were leaving.

This time our own mission's organization and Bob Mason were the ones who appeared to withhold valuable information from us and had secrets of their own.

Chapter 9

A Welcome Diversion

After saying our goodbyes to our new friend, Lupita, we began our arduous drive back to Bacalar. The drive was a quiet one. Seeing the dusty turnoff and military post four miles outside of town actually brought relief to us all. Driving south toward our house, we enjoyed the beautiful blue water of the lake. We rolled the windows down and let the coastal winds move through the truck. The lake, its color, and the breeze made for an intoxicating potion.

As we approached the house, the gate swung open. The *valador* was mowing the emerald green lawn with his sharpened machete. *Swoosh, swoosh* went the blade, back and forth across the yard in a methodical manner: laborious, but efficient. We were glad to be home. Our chalky white-colored house sat on a beautiful lawn and overlooked the multi-colored lake. The bottom of the lake was lime, which made the aquamarine water crystal clear. Palm trees flanked the yard on both sides of the rock wall that surrounded the property. It was truly a gorgeous place. In better circumstances it would be just a touch of heaven.

The interior of our home was not so striking. Although beautiful, marbled Mexican tile decorated every floor, the furnishings were meager. In the den, an army green cot served as our sofa. We had that and a small, 15-inch TV we had recently bought in Belize. The den also housed our computer. The kitchen was sparsely equipped with two pots, one skillet, and a small selection of can goods. We counted our lucky stars because we did have a refrigerator. A small kitchen table and chairs were brought from Plano. Upstairs were three bedrooms and a bath. Each of the rooms bore weary mattresses and floor fans. The few clothes that we did own were kept in large, blue storage bins. Up another set of stairs brought you to the roof, where we washed and hung our clothes out to dry. Not exactly living in the lap of luxury, but comfortable.

After showing Andy and Heidi to their room, we met downstairs to regroup. Andy called the *abagado*, or lawyer, to set up a meeting. We had several hours before meeting the lawyer, so we decided to have a late lunch/early dinner. Vico's Pizzeria made a mean "Mexican/Italian" pizza! We ordered a large combination, which included sausage, cheese, and Canadian bacon (ham). Sitting on the front porch under a fan and sipping soft drinks, the moments of laughter felt invigorating and rejuvenated my spirit. For the first time in weeks, I actually had an appetite. Visiting and actually enjoying a meal with friends: how long had it been since Mike and I had done that? An eternity, we believed.

Soon we were on our way to the lawyer's house. As we pulled up to his quaint, Spanish abode, Juan greeted us with smiles and the obligatory kiss on each cheek. We were escorted out to the back veranda which overlooked the lake. In moments, Juan heard our story and offered his assistance. On his suggestion, we went back to the restaurant to question Yamelle once again.

As we approached, Yamelle became unnerved at the site of Juan. The two spoke in Spanish for a few minutes. Yamelle evidently had been withholding information from us. Aldo had actually spoken with her a few days before. She slipped and told Juan he was staying at Hotel Hacienda in Mexico City.

"Mexico City?" I whispered, "How are we ever going to find them there?" Well, at least now we had a new lead. That was good, right? Juan planned to leave the next morning. He promised to call us with any new information he collected. We gave him 5,000 *pesos* for expenses. He was to return to Bacalar in four days. We said our goodbyes and became encouraged once again.

The emotional rollercoaster was taking its toll on both Mike and me. One moment we would be in the pit of hell, shaking and lost. The next minute (or so it seemed) we would be filled with hope and anticipation—a difficult way to live. The human body is not meant to survive under such extreme pressure for very long. We were normal people. We had not been through combat training or terrorist training. We were reacting to every moment, to every piece of information that was given to us: up . . . down . . . up . . . down . . . the cycle continued at a daunting pace.

That night sleep washed over us all. But sleeping for me never lasted long. I awoke at 4 a.m. and played countless games of solitaire on the computer before the rest of the house awoke at 7. Andy and Mike decided to go to the clinic site after breakfast. Heidi and I stayed behind. Heidi sat on the army cot. I sat on the only chair we owned—a folding chair.

Sitting and waiting can be a laborious process. After about an hour, Heidi began to cry. I looked at her and asked with surprise, "Heidi, what's the matter?"

Tears filled her eyes as she hugged her fit, tan legs. She brushed her auburn hair from her beautiful brown face and said, "I can't stand it. How do you do it? At least I know where Tanner is."

With that, tears filled my eyes. I rushed to sit down beside her. "I don't know how I go on," I said. "I'm tired of being strong. I want this to be over."

I was so humbled. Here Heidi was crying for me. She had lost her son—a son that was never returning to her. We held each other for a long while. Both of us had experienced great loss; both had heartache. We shared a bond that nothing could penetrate.

The sun's afternoon rays encroached into the den, so we went outside and sat in the tropical breeze. Neighbors played and splashed in the blue water while we sat and basked in the warm sun. Once again the warm rays reminded me that I was alive. Conversation was not important—the mere company of having another human being beside me and sharing my pain, even for a moment, was so comforting.

As evening fell, Mike's truck pulled into the drive. On the way home he and Andy had stopped at "Pollo Ensanda." This place fixed the best outdoor barbecue chicken I have ever tasted. Our dinner consisted of barbecue chicken, handmade tortillas, *pico de gallo*, Mexican rice, black beans with fresh cilantro, and *creama*, the wonderful condiment that was like sour cream but not refrigerated. It is a little taste of heaven! *Anna and the King* was the movie of choice to watch on video. Wow, there we were, sitting in our den, having dinner and a watching a movie with friends, like normal folks. We felt good to be ordinary for a moment.

Our morning brought sadness. Andy and Heidi needed to go back home. After all, they had a family and a life to which they needed to return. After breakfast Mike made the long and monotonous trip to Cancun and back. It was necessary and would take all day. After saying our sad goodbyes, our friends were on their way back to normal life. I was stuck in hell.

Chapter 10

Misplaced Loyalties

Mike drove into the driveway around 3:30 in the afternoon. While he drove back from Cancun alone, he had had time to think. He entered the house with a quickened pace. He began, "Vanda, I have an idea. If we can locate the phone number of the restaurant, then we can check all of the incoming and outgoing calls."

I was confused. "Why would we do that?" I inquired.

"Well, maybe we can see how many times Aldo has been in contact with Yamelle and where he called her from," he added.

"Sounds like a plan to me!" I said. "Let's do it!"

A new surge of energy filled the truck as we drove to Chetumal. We drove up to the phone store and entered Aldo's phone number into the machine. The main purpose of this machine is to enable someone to pay his phone bill without having to wait in the long line inside the store itself. As far as I can tell, this machine is uniquely Mexican. It has no security. Anyone can walk up to the large machine and enter a phone number. Magically a phone log appears.

We decided to get the phone records for the past four months. My heart beat wildly. I was excited. We waited in the scorching heat. The machine spat out five pages of communication for the restaurant.

"Were they ever in Cancun?" was my first question to Mike. We sat in the truck and began to look over the statement.

"Look, Vanda. Aldo began calling Alejandra in Argentina right after we arrived," Mike said. "It shows no calls to Argentina until after our arrival in Bacalar. He called her every day for eight days. Some phone calls were almost two-hours long."

With a cursory glance we noticed that it showed no calls to or from Cancun, so all of that time we spent in Cancun was basically wasted. "They were NEVER IN CANCUN!" Mike exclaimed. We were beginning to realize that we had been duped!

On the way home, I drove while Mike continued to study the records. The list showed several phone calls to and from Mexico City, just as Yamelle stated.

"Juan might find this information interesting," Mike said. On returning home we called Juan and gave him the mystery phone numbers from Mexico City. Juan and Mike spoke on the phone for a few minutes. After they exchanged information, Mike hung up the phone. We were hoping against hope Juan would be able to match the phone numbers with the establishment.

Juan called the next afternoon. He had news. "I went to the hotel today," Juan told Mike. "I showed the pictures you gave me to a few people in the hotel. The maid said that all three of them were here but that they checked out this morning," he continued.

"What?" Mike replied. "How could you have missed them?" he questioned.

"I'll stay another day and see if I can spot them," Juan said. "But don't get your hopes up. Yamelle probably alerted them to my conversation with her," he continued

Another disappointment. Now we had to confront another question. Did Brittany go with them voluntarily? My mind did not want to go there. If she went voluntarily, then why had she

90

not told us the truth to begin with? Why did she tell us that she was not with them and that SHE WAS TRAVELING ALONE? That notion made no sense to either of us. More to the story surely existed, but again, we had been left out of the loop and had no daughter.

Nightfall brought quietness and more waiting. In the silence of the evening, Mike and I grew weary.

"I'm going to check our email," Mike said.

"OK, but she hasn't emailed us, I checked today three times already!" I responded in a dejected voice.

Mike logged on and BAM! An email from Brittany. It began:

Mom & Dad:

I am fine. I am traveling alone. No one is with me.
I don't know why you said such bad things about Aldo.
He is not bad. He is nice. I want to be by myself.
I do not want to go to school.
I do not want you to look for me.
I will come home when I want to.

Love,
Brittany

Mike and I stared at the computer screen. My heart was heavy with hurt and a longing to see my daughter.

"Mike, this is not her," I said. "Or is it?" I questioned. My mind was so full of uncertainty. I didn't know what to think.

Mike's eyes filled with tears as he sat in front of the screen and did not know what to do next. "Do we keep looking for her, Vanda, or do we give up like she asks?" he whispered.

"We keep looking," I said as I leaned over and kissed his ebony, curly head. My eyes filled with tears. My heart was breaking in two. Our world had been turned upside down.

We did not hear from Juan again. Days trickled by like a slow rain—*drip-drop, drip-drop*. Juan returned from the trip, but he never called to give us an update. We drove by his house numerous times, but he avoided us.

"What now?" we thought. "Let's drive by there one more time," Mike said. He tried to sound optimistic. Juan was there, but he refused to speak to us and disallowed us entry onto his property.

"Something must have happened in Mexico City, Vanda" Mike said. "I'm going to call Andy and see if Juan will talk with him," he continued.

Andy called us back in a few hours with sad news. Juan became evasive about his adventure to Mexico City. Andy had to coax him quite a bit before he was able to hear even the slightest hint of the truth.

Andy finagled the story out of Juan. Something did in fact happen in Mexico City. Evidently Juan spotted Aldo and confronted him. Scared of being caught but holding some extra cash, apparently Aldo paid him off. Wow, Mexicans sure did have an odd sense of right and wrong. Money evidently was more important to Juan than doing what he was hired to do.

Andy was apologetic for even recommending Juan in the first place.

"Andy, we would never have this information if it weren't for him. Don't be sorry. At least we know that they are together and they were in Mexico City," Mike said with sadness in his voice. He hung up the phone.

Mike walked toward me and gently wrapped his strong arms around me. I wanted to melt into him and never return. A chill ran through me despite the heat. A foreboding gloom returned.

"Now what?" Mike said.

We had no leads and nowhere to turn. We were running out of money and longed to go home: back to Plano to be with our friends and family. We longed for the comfort of friendly faces and arms—arms we could trust. But here we were: stuck in the filthy mire, in the pits of a hellish inferno, tangled in a web of lies and deceit.

Days passed with no word from Brittany—no word from anyone. We did not know where to turn next. The days were long, but the nights were worse. Each night was torment for me. Sleep was long in overtaking me. I would wait for it to envelop my mind and my body. Each night I would doze into slumber only to wake with a most horrific nightmare. The dream was always the same.

In my dream there was a stark, white phone on a table draped with a black, billowy fabric. It stood in the middle of a shadowy, dark hallway. A small light from above illuminated the lone device on the table. A foggy mist billowed up from under and around the table. Utter darkness surrounded the area. The phone was ringing and ringing. It echoed through the long, dark passage. I envisioned myself running to get the phone, but the faster I ran, the farther the phone would move away from me into obscurity. The phone's piercing ring would wake me from my sleep. I would begin frantically running down the stairs fast as lightening to reach our phone. But as I reached for the receiver, I awoke into a rational state only to realize that the phone was not ringing. No one was there.

Night after night, the phone lay silent. Brittany's sweet voice saying, "Mom, I love you. Find me!" was not there: only a droning dial tone. Adrenaline flowed through my weak body and caused my heart to race. Dazed, I would return to bed and lie awake trembling with terror over the dream. The ghostly, haunting dream returned nightly. Soon I dreaded even trying to go to sleep because I feared the dream's return.

Chapter 11

Help from Cartoonland

In those dreadful days I was so thankful that the Lord had taught me to be still. Stillness and rest are required to hear God's voice. God's address is stillness.

Psalm 37 states that one must *be still before the Lord and wait patiently for Him.* However, this Scripture became increasingly more difficult to hang on. My mind knew that anger and fretting only led to evil, but my heart grew anxious. Nonetheless, we waited on the Lord for some kind of direction as we knew in our spirits that He would not *forsake us nor abandon us* in our agony.

By Saturday we were out of food and in dire need of some staples. I was off to the store. *I wish Mike would go*, I thought. *I don't want to eat anything.* But even if only for a few moments, it distracted me from thinking about our circumstances.

As I entered the market, a man in a grubby, ancient, gold Plymouth pulled up beside me. Smoking a cigarette with his left arm hanging out of the window, the man leaned out of the car and whispered, "Hey, aren't you the American lady that lost her daughter?"

Intrigued, I walked over to the car, "Yes, I am," I said.

"Well, I am an ex-CIA agent. I think I can help you find her," he said in a clandestine voice. He darted his head from side to side as if he were afraid that someone was watching us.

"O-k-a-y," I said with a certain degree of skepticism. "I'll come down to your house in about an hour," he said.

"OK," I said. "We live out of town about . . ."

"Yeah, lady, I know where you live. Everyone knows where you live," he announced.

"Wow!" I thought. "Now that's pretty creepy!" In a cloud of smoke, he was gone.

My heart beat quickly with great anticipation once again. "Thank You, God, I knew You would bring someone to help us," I whispered quietly to God.

Hurriedly I gather a few items at the store and went back home to relay the news to Mike. Running into the house, I found Mike napping on the couch (cot). A strong breeze that blew off the blue water made the house quite comfortable. I began, "Mike, wake up! I met a man at the market; he's going to help us find Brittany."

Waking slowly, Mike said, "Slow down, Vanda, and tell me what you're talking about."

"OK, there's a guy coming here in about 20 minutes. He said he could help us find Brittany. He's an ex-CIA agent. He has all sorts of contacts and ways of gathering information," I recounted in a quick voice. "Maybe this could be the answer to our prayers," I said with excitement.

If something sounds too good to be true, it probably is. But, we were not thinking rationally at this point!

Moments later, the Plymouth pulled into the drive. Two men got out. Mike opened the door and said, "Hi, I'm Mike."

"I'm Alan. This is my friend, Phillip," Alan said as they walked into the house. Both were smoking cigarettes.

Alan wore dirty sandals, long khaki shorts, and no shirt. Yuck! His pudgy, tan belly hung over his shorts. His sandy, reddish hair was peppered with strands of gray and was in dire need of a trim. His worn face revealed a difficult life. He must have been about 50.

I don't want them smoking in my house, I thought. *On second thought, if they can find Brittany, I don't really care.*

Phillip was from the Netherlands and once worked with the KGB (or so he said). Phillip stood about 6-foot-4 and wore black jeans, a torn blue T-shirt, and no shoes. His milky white skin only called attention to his translucent blue eyes and dirty brown hair. This was quite a pair. They looked like two characters out of a cartoon strip.

Alan ranted for almost an hour about his background in the CIA, why he left, and why no one—not even our family—could know that he was helping us, not even our family. Boy, now that sounded like some top-secret stuff to me.

"We'll work from your house," Alan said. "Phillip will go and get his computer and other gear that we'll need. He'll stay in a room upstairs, because he often will be working all hours of the night," he continued.

Phillip was going to install a program on our computer so no one could hack into it. "Black Ice" would be installed, along with a tracking device on the phone so if Brittany called, we could trace where her call came from, or so we thought. We had to remember that this was Mexico; nothing worked as it was supposed to.

The men left. Our heads were spinning. "Mike," I began, do you really think that they can find her? What are they going to do?"

"Well, for one thing, Phillip knows how to check the IP addresses on the emails we have received from Brittany," he said."Beyond that, I'm not sure.

Several hours later Alan and Phillip returned with boxes and boxes of wires, speakers, printers, computers, scanners, and other stuff. Our house looked like a command post or something out of a hostage movie. I was hoping something would work as a result of all of this mumbo jumbo.

After about two days of Phillip's working around the clock, with only minimal sleep, we had a lead. Phillip had been tracking the IP addresses from the emails. Scratching his head and smoking a cigarette, Phillip began, "Three emails seem to be from the same IP address."

"What does that mean?" I asked with amazement.

"It means that these three emails all came from the same business," he said.

"Wow, really?" I inquired. "What's next, guys?"

Alan piped up. "We're going to Mexico City and find her."

"What? Oh, great. This is AWESOME!"

Man, this was easier than we thought. If only the process could have been as easy as it seemed!

All three men began to pack for the 18-hour drive to Mexico City. Mike drove into Chetumal to the ATM machine for money, as we had to bear all of the financial responsibility. While Alan and Phillip did not expect to gain financially from this endeavor, they did expect that all of their expenses would be covered.

Finally at 11 p.m. everything was ready. "Vanda, will you be OK here by yourself?" Mike asked.

We lived four miles south of town. They were taking our only mode of transportation: the big red truck.

"Yeah, I'll be fine. Just call me and let me know what you find out."

Mike pulled me into him and held me tight. *Don't let go*, I thought. But Alan motioned that they needed to leave. They pulled out of the driveway. The house grew silent. I hoped they would return. Mexico City is only the biggest and scariest city in the world. Law enforcement is corrupt; gangs control much of the city. I was terrified I might never see Mike again either.

My spirit was filled with angst. It was midnight, but as usual, I could not sleep. Many times during the next month my moral fiber would be put into the "refiner's fire." Darlene

Zschech's praise and worship tape went into the video player. Soon praise and love replaced the trepidation and fear that had invaded my spirit. My fear had dissipated; my soul was calm.

I can do this, I told myself. Alone for at least five days, I began to pray. "Lord, give me strength, I can do it," I repeated with doubt in my voice. I climbed the stairs and waited for sleep to visit my body—sleep and the everpresent dream about the telephone and Brittany. They returned.

Morning brought new hope. I could sense the Lord's presence in the house. God is so BIG in His infinite wisdom. His purposes are always revealed at the perfect moment. He taught me to be still. Had I not learned this lesson, at least to some degree, I would have gone crazy after only 30 minutes of being alone. My day would be a lot of being still and waiting: solitaire and coffee at 5 a.m., pasta at noon, reading in the Mayan sun until 5 p.m., and then a walk in the evening breeze. As twilight fell, I ate Mexican *sopa* and watched *Anna and the King* for the 100th time. Aaron Jeffries' *He Is* played on the CD all day. Day one passed. No word from Mike. Darkness fell; the dream returned.

Day one rolled into day two. Mike called to say that they arrived safely. Alan and Phillip had a plan. Revealing no details of the plan, Mike's sweet voice was gone. Whatever it was, I hoped it would work. We needed something to hang onto.

Just then, when things looked bleak, God's hand delivered a valentine in the form of a phone call from my mom. My mom was a real Southern lady, if ever one existed. Mom to me, or Margaret Hester to the rest of the world, is a Southern lady from Georgia. Her accent dripped like peaches in heavy syrup; her manners were impeccable, every outfit was coordinated, and every hair was in place. If ever you're in need, Margaret is one to call! She is my steel magnolia.

Mom and I had been staying in touch. She served as my strong tower during much of this whole ordeal. In fact she worried about the toll all of this was having on my mental state. She sensed my frustration and began to take matters into her own hands. She was a woman of action. She began working quietly behind the scenes on my behalf.

Day two segued into day three. The silence was deafening, the isolation unbearable. The hours of each day were spent much like those the day before had been. I needed to talk to a human being—someone I loved and cared about. So I called my son, Chris.

"Mom, I can't believe you are there by yourself. How well do you know these guys dad went with?" he inquired.

"Not very well. We only met them a few days ago," I said as I sensed doubt in Chris's voice. "How do you know you can trust them? You trusted Aldo. Look what happened," he said.

MAN, I hate it when he's right, I said to myself. "Yeah, Chris, you're right, I know, but Dad's gone now. Let's just hope everything turns out OK," I said as I tried to convince myself.

"OK, Mom, I'll lay off. Just don't be so trusting of everyone," he said with tenderness in his voice.

Chris possessed a sixth-sense. His genuine nature enabled him to see through a person's character. His candid look at the world allowed him to see people as they really are. We said our goodbyes. I lay the receiver gently back on the phone. Boy, I missed his wit and brazen ways.

"Next time he volunteers to rescue us, I'm going to take him up on it!" I thought as I clung to Chris's sweet voice.

Chapter 12

The Well Runs Deep

I walked out into the cloudless day. Strolling down to the property's edge, I stepped off into the cool, crystal water. The soft, lime bottom of the lake felt good between my toes. Lapping waves slapped against the pier. A languid breeze blew. The property was situated on the lake in such a way that from the pier, one could see forever. I sat in the sun for hours as I listened to praise and worship music and felt alive. One of my favorite songs, "Butterfly", lifted my spirits. The words reminded me of Brittany: *Fly, fly butterfly fly. Stand upon these two shoulders of mine. Spread those wings of yours and fly . . .*

I possessed such dreams for Brittany. As her parents, Mike and I wanted to help her realize her potential. "Brittany," I would say, "You can be anything you want . . . a teacher, a doctor, a lawyer . . . your dad and I just want you to be happy." I prayed for a precious daughter—one who one day would spread her wings and fly. The lyrics of the song, the warm sun, and the gentle waves lulled me to sleep.

The phone rang. I jumped. Running into the house, I whispered, "Maybe it's Mike." Longing to hear his voice, I picked up the receiver. "Hello," I said.

"Mom, hey, Mom, what 'cha doin'?" It was Brittany! My mind began to race. *OK, stay calm. Don't make her upset. Keep her on the phone*, I told myself with determination.

"Hey, Brittany," I said with a tremor in my voice. "Where are you?" I asked. "How are you? I miss you. Are you OK?"

Stop it! I heard myself say, but I couldn't help it. The questions kept popping out of my big mouth. "When are you coming home? Are you still with Aldo and Alejandra?" I continued with tears streaming down my flushed cheeks.

My heart was breaking in two. I wanted to reach into the phone and pull her through the receiver. *Oh, God, I can't get to her*, I thought.

"I'm NOT traveling with them any more," she said with anger in her voice. "I'm fine, Mom. I'm traveling around Mexico on a bus. I've always wanted to see Mexico," she said. "Is Dad there?" she asked.

What do I tell her? I questioned myself. "He's gone to Chetumal for the day to pick up some things for Rosie," I said.

"OK, I wanted to talk to him. I love you. I'll talk to you soon. Bye."

"Wait, Brittany, where . . . when . . . why . . .?" The phone was dead. In an instant she was gone. Dumfounded, I stood in the middle of the den. I clutched the phone and trembled with anger. My head reeled with confusion. I felt as though I had been struck by lightning.

I recalled the conversation, such as it was. She told me nothing EXCEPT A LIE. Her voice was light and happy. She did not cry when I cried. My mind grew weary trying to decipher her stories. "We know she's not traveling around Mexico. We know that she's with Aldo and Alejandra. We know that they are in Mexico City," I said to the stark white wall as I paced around the room. More confused than ever, I sat down on the floor and wept. I prayed. I wept. I wanted to die.

I closed my eyes and began, "Please Father, pass this cup from me. I can't do this any more. I'm done. I'm confused. I'm hurt. I'm exhausted. No more. I can't take any more. Please, Father." Lying on the floor broken and exhausted, I felt Him place His arms around me.

"Be still," I felt Him say. Lean on Me, I AM," he whispered to my spirit.

Some how I managed to pull it together. *Mike. I want to talk to Mike*, I thought. I called. No reception! I hated Mexico. I had to WAIT until he called me. The afternoon trudged at a turtle's pace. I returned back to my chair in the sun, listened to Nicole C. Mullins sing "On My Knees" and lifted up the Lord through worship. My spirit was sad, but I knew I had to lean on Him. I could not carry this.

Evening fell. I returned to the still and lonely den and waited on Mike's call.

At 9:30 p.m. the phone rang. My heart jumped. "Hello," I said.

"Vanda, it's Mom. Are you OK?" she asked in her mother voice.

"Mom," I began as my heart began to race, "Brittany called today." I told her about the conversation. I hated to tell her. Mom thought Brittany left on her own. I was not ready to even entertain that idea. Not yet. Mom sensed the tension and changed the subject. *Smart lady.*

"I've written another email to Sam Johnson," she stated. "I lived in Texas for 20 some-odd years. He'd better answer me," she threatened. When Mom got passionate about something, she would not let it go. Her strength remained a silent force. Her passion for helping me remained undaunted.

She wrote Texas Sen. Kay Bailey Hutchison and Sam Johnson, our U.S. representatives from the Plano area. Her Southern idealist mind hoped that one of these two governmental representatives could help us. Mom emailed Kay Bailey Hutchison more than three times. Each letter was responded to with a canned and ready reply. "Thank you for your email. We are sorry, but we can not help you." Sam Johnson's office was no better. Disheartening as it may seem, the same representatives that we elect and vote into office have important and pressing matters to attend to—much more important than a missing 15-year-old girl. I have longed to ask each of them, "What if your daughter was missing? Would you have time then?"

Being a proud American, I love my country and have always supported it through good times and bad. Now, for the first time in my life, I needed my country and believed my elected officials had turned their backs on me. It hurt. I was crushed. *Is this what being an American means?* I wondered. This was a reality check for which I was not ready.

I was relieved to have my mom in my court. I was glad to have a distraction from the unnerving isolation. Hours passed; still no call from Mike. After my conversation with Chris, I worried that something would go wrong.

Finally, Mike called at last. We spent time discussing Brittany's phone conversation from earlier in the day.

Mike appeared to be as flustered and confused as I was. "Vanda, I don't care what she says. We are looking for her until we can see with our own eyes that she is OK," he said.

"I agree," I softly whispered. "Mike, it was just so horrible. If I could have just pulled her through the phone . . . ."

Then with a sigh, I asked, "What did you guys find out?"

"We went to the Internet café where the emails were sent. The man recognized Aldo and Brittany, but that's all," he stated. "The owner hasn't seen them for several days," he added.

"Which means what?" I asked.

"That they could have moved again," Mike said.

More disappointment hit us in the face. As the men had set out for Mexico City, we were so hopeful that they would just sit across from the café, watch for Brittany to enter, and then take her. No such luck. With no leads once again, the men decided to return home and regroup.

Chapter 13

Lies that Pierce the Soul

Once home, we tried to work out another plan of action. Once again, the Lord revealed His sovereign hand. The phone rang. It was Ernestina, the head reporter from the Cancun newspaper. She had just received a letter from Brittany. It was sent to the American Consulate in Merida. She faxed us a copy of the letter. It read:

Dearest Ms. Ernestina:

Thank you so much for all of your concern for me. I am fine.
There is no need to worry about me.
I ran away from home before and was gone for 4 days.
They found me, but I did not want to live with them.
My parents are very bad people. They hurt me.
Please don't help them anymore.

Signed,
Brittany Terrell

As the fax rolled off the machine, my heart raced. *Hurry up*, I thought. Dying to read the letter, Mike and I huddled over the flimsy white sheet bearing the text. Her handwriting was horrible.

Before we could finish the letter, Ernestina called back. Mike picked up the receiver. He began, "Yes, we received the letter." He continued, "When did you get this? Where did you get it? Ernestina, none of this is true. Well . . . yes, she did run away once before. She was mad because she was grounded. She couldn't go out. She was gone for four days."

Ernestina asked if she could visit us in Bacalar the next day. Brittany's letter had only thrown suspicion on Mike and me and had left Ernestina with questions of her own.

"Sure," Mike said and hung up the phone. Mike and I had nothing to hide. We knew we were good people. Now we had only to convince the entire country of Mexico.

Totally stunned by this new piece of the puzzle, we stood staring at each other's zombie-like faces. My body was numb, devoid of any human emotion. I just stood there staring at Mike. *How could she do this? Could anything possibly happen to hurt us any more than this lie?*

"Mike," I said as I woke from my zombie state, "She just told the whole country that her mom and dad are very bad people." As the words emerged from my mouth . . . *very bad people* . . . anger sprang up inside me. "What made her say that about us?" I asked. More questions surfaced. Once again, we had no clue where to search for the answers.

"She KNOWS we're not BAD people." We sat on the sofa. Too numb to feel or talk, I just wept softly, as I realized that the nightmare was stuck in rewind mode and would never end.

Alan and Phillip arrived. We all began to dissect the letter. Unable to believe that our own daughter could actually be this cruel, I was grasping at straws. "Could she be trying to send us some kind of secret message?" I asked. Trying to make sense of it all I said, "Sometimes people do that when they have been kidnapped. They try and send a message through their words," I continued.

Because of our desperate state we scoured the letter looking for clues and even made up connections.

After several hours of going over the letter, we decided that the letter was what it was. But we still couldn't grasp why she said what she did. My mind was exhausted, my body numb. The pain was almost unbearable. With each piece of news I felt like a spring being wound tighter and tighter. I was unable to escape—unable to release the building tension even if only for a moment.

The phone rang. Chris was calling. Mike talked to him and told Chris about the fax. With determination Chris said, "Dad, I'm flying down there. I'll call you when I make the arrangements. YOU'RE NOT TALKING ME OUT OF THIS. My mind is made up! I'm doing this no matter what you say!"

"OK, Chris," Mike began. "We want you here. We need you. Your mom needs you. Call me. I'll pick you up at the airport."

As Mike hung up the phone, he looked at me. I broke down.

"When?" I asked with tears rolling down my cheeks.

"Soon, Vanda," Mike said as he pulled me into him. *My son wants to be with us, to hold me and support us.* The relief was incredible.

Mike and I held each other for a long time. I didn't want to let go. I felt so safe in his arms. Alan and Phillip sensed that we wanted to be alone and decided to leave and return again in the morning. For the first time in several weeks Mike and I had the house to ourselves.

We walked upstairs to rest our weary bodies. Our hearts were broken and our spirits exhausted. Like a welcomed friend sleep enveloped us and freed our minds momentarily.

Ernestina arrived at around 11 the next morning. I picked up Rosie in case she needed to translate. Ernestina spoke English; however, her thick accent often proved too difficult for the untrained ear. When she spoke quickly, it became almost impossible to understand her.

After exchanging hellos, she began, "I want to ask you about the items Brittany outlined in her letter. Can you tell me if Brittany has ever run away?"

"Yes," Mike said. "When she was 13, Brittany was grounded for the day but wanted to go to the mall with her friends. We said *no*. She could not go. After she pouted in her room for an hour, she asked if she could go down the street and play with David and Sarah, two kids she had started babysitting after school. We said *OK*. She left. Hours went by and Brittany had not returned. Worried, Vanda called David and Sarah's mom. Brittany was not there. She had never gone to their house. Several hours went by before the phone rang

"It was Brittany," Mike continued. "Brittany began trying to spin a new tale as to why she had not returned home, but Vanda told Brittany that she knew she was not down the street with the kids. Brittany was scared about being caught in a lie. She knew she would be in trouble, so she didn't return home. Some of her friends picked her up. They went out for a joy ride. Upon their return, the car had a flat tire. She ended up in Garland, with no way to get home and no feasible story to tell us, so she just never returned home. Our youth pastor found her four days later at some guy's house."

"It was torture not knowing where she was." I said. "I thought we were never going to find her," I continued. "That's why she ran away. We're not sure if she would have ever returned if we had not found her."

As we sat in the small den recounting this story of Brittany's earlier disappearance, I began reliving that ordeal all over again. The sleepless nights full of tears and questions as to her whereabouts back then flooded my mind. I kept asking myself, *Where is she? Did her friends have any idea where she was or who she was with?* With this, I lay on the floor prostrate and prayed for her safety. I cried a million tears.

Feeling guilty because I had confronted her on the phone, I searched her room for any minute clue as to whom she might be with. I found several dozen pieces of torn paper in hidden places. We called every number we found. Some of the numbers were from strangers. We left no stone unturned, but we basically had no idea where she was or with whom she was staying. Mike and felt as if we couldn't go on.

I now realize that God was warning us about what could happen: a current nightmare more ghoulish than one could imagine: a lurid tale full of uncertainties and heartache. I know it sounds strange, but now, sitting in our den in Mexico, I felt a comfort of sorts to have a glimpse of God's love and His sovereign hand. Back then He was preparing us for future heartache. Without our enduring Brittany's previous disappearance and return, I doubt if I would have ever had the strength to endure the past months of hell. It just reminds me that our Father knows all things and that all who are in Christ know that God guides our every step.

Ernestina seemed satisfied with our response and moved on to the dreaded question. "Why would she say that you are very bad people?" she asked.

I began to tremble as the words emerged from her mouth. "I don't know," I said with my head in my hands, "I honestly don't know why she would ever say that."

"Do you think she is still with Aldo and his daughter?" she asked. Mike told her about his trip to Mexico City and that we had reason to believe that the three of them were still together.

"OK," Ernestina said. "My heart breaks for you. I really want to help. You seem like nice people." An hour passed before Ernestina said she needed to return to Cancun. Before she left, she promised to do everything possible to help us.

With Rosie still in tow, back to the restaurant we went to speak with Yamelle. Mike wanted to confront her again and pump her for information. As we walked up to the outside bar area, Yamelle's mouth turned to a sinister grin. Her pleasant demeanor quickly transformed into that of an aloof, wicked woman—a woman without compassion or love.

As Rosie approached Yamelle, she inquired *"Buenos.* Have you spoken with Aldo?" Yamelle did not answer but instead bent down under the counter and pulled out a magazine called *TV Notas,* a celebrity-focused entertainment publication printed in Spanish. With great anticipation she coldly flipped the magazine open.

Looking at our faces she revealed a two-page article about Brittany. It was complete with pictures from the modeling shoot. Disgust and shock filled our bodies.

"What in the world?" I began but quickly noticed that Yamelle was enjoying this way too much. I struggled to read the article in Spanish. The author of the article began by stating that he spotted Brittany wandering around Six Flags (in Mexico City) and just asked if he could talk with her.

As I glared at Yamelle, I wondered, *How could this woman be so evil and vindictive? She loves the pain this is causing us.* I grabbed the magazine as Yamelle spoke rapidly in Spanish and retold the high points.

"Rosie," I began. "Please tell us what the article says," I asked as my body trembled with fear.

Rosie began, "It says that Brittany was vacationing in Cancun with her parents and that she ran away from them." She continued, "It states that Brittany has a huge inheritance from her grandmother that the two of you are living off of. It then states that her father has molested her numerous times." Rosie then pointed to a picture of Brittany highlighting a big scar on her foot and said, "And this is where her father shot her while she was trying to escape an attack." In truth, the scar was from an infected mosquito bite. But it did not appear anyone cared too much about the truth!

"What?" I screamed. Rosie continued, "It says here that she has a small scar on her forehead where Vanda threw an ashtray across the room, hit her in the head, and knocked her unconscious." (This was also preposterous.)

"Oh, my gosh," I said. "I'm not believing this." We looked at the magazine and noticed the same letter that had been sent to Ernestina was down in the bottom right-hand corner of the article.

"The article concludes by begging the Mexican people not to help you because you are bad people," Rosie said.

Mike and I were in complete and utter shock. What else could possible thwart our efforts to find Brittany? My knees were shaking; my stomach once again felt as though it had been seared with a hot knife. The child, the long-awaited daughter that we longed for, is saying these things about us? It was more than a body could stand.

"What now?" Mike asked.

"I don't know," I said. I was so broken, I had no idea which way was up anymore. I tried to remain standing. Holding back from Yamelle the tears and the disappointment took superhuman strength. I didn't want to give her the satisfaction she was seeking: to see me fall into a heap on the ground.

Memories of our precious Brittany began to flood my mind. Memories of her playing dress-up . . . she loved her red, white, and blue cheerleading costume the best. And in an instant . . . she rode her bike for the first time without training wheels; she beamed with pride as the small bike swerved back and forth. And then the most precious memory of all . . . her falling asleep on the sofa, with her little arms wrapped around our blonde cocker spaniel, Bobo.

If only I could hold her one more time, I thought. But my thoughts were interrupted by angry words.

Yamelle ranted loudly, "This is Aldo. This sounds just like something he would do." Her sinister smile hid just under the surface. We could tell that Yamelle was quite pleased at our pained response. Stunned, broken, and bewildered, we left the restaurant in search of our own copy of the magazine article.

As the day closed, Alan and Phillip returned. We showed them the *TV Notas* article. Again we racked our brains for some type of plan. Phillip looked at the fax Ernestina sent us.

Ernestina, I thought with hope. *She should be back at the station by now. I'm going to call and tell her about the article.* I dialed the number but was met with, "She is not available," her assistant said coldly. Ernestina never returned our calls. We never heard from her again. She, like many others, most likely believed the lies about us. Our daughter, making the pain almost unbearable, defamed our character. Ernestina, once an ally, now magically dried up like a parched oak leaf.

Dissecting the minuscule lettering at the top of the fax, Phillip searched for a pattern. With the mind of a private eye, Phillip began deciphering the code. It was a phone number where the fax had been sent. A lead. Phillip began working his magic at the computer.

After an hour of searching he found a place of business matching the phone number. It was in Mexico City and was located in the same zone as Six Flags. "Maybe they are living somewhere around there," Phillip said.

"I think we should go see if we can find her," Alan added.

Mike and I were so weary. We didn't know what to think. We weren't thinking too straight. The guys talked through the new leads we had. They decided to depart once again and leave me alone again for days by myself.

Oh, no, I thought. *I don't know if I can do this again.* But I put on my brave face and said, "Whatever you guys think is best." They were off within the hour.

As the sun set the next day, Mike called to say that they had arrived. He decided to go by himself and visit the American Embassy. Mike wanted to talk with the embassy about helping us find Brittany. At the beginning of our search we hadn't considered going to the embassy, because we thought we would find Brittany in a few days, but that hadn't happened. We now had quite a few pieces of evidence that pointed to Aldo and Mexico City. Mike was sure the embassy would help! After all, they were part of our government.

Alan thought they should first go to the police station. The three men entered the station. Alan, with his clandestine persona, said he would do all of the talking (big mistake). The police began asking questions of their own as to Alan's identity. Alan's evasiveness and cryptic answers only threw more suspicion on the men.

They left the station and made their way to the business where the fax had been sent. From a photo the owner of the establishment recognized Brittany and Alejandra. *OK, that was that. Now what?* Mike questioned to himself.

Then he told Alan that he wanted to go to the American Embassy alone. Alan was not keen on the idea, but he agreed. Alan and Phillip waited at a coffee shop down the street.

On Mike's arrival, he was ushered into an office, in which he waited for a long while. After speaking to several people Mike was escorted to the director's office. Mike began to tell Mr. Ramirez about our plight. The agent listened intently. The meeting lasted well over an hour.

When Mike finished speaking, the man reached into a drawer and pulled out the *TV Notas* article. "What about this article?" the man inquired.

"It's not true," Mike began. "Our daughter must have been coerced into writing those things. She loves us."

"How do I know what you're telling me is the truth and not what's written here?" the agent asked.

"Because I'm her father; I'm trying to find her," Mike said in desperation.

Doubt and a cold sneer appeared over the man's face as he stood up. Holding out his hand, he began, "Well, thank you, Mr. Terrell, for visiting. I'll see what I can do."

As Mike walked down the marble steps of the austere building, he realized that the article was going to haunt us at every turn. Mike replayed the meeting and felt that Mr. Ramirez didn't exactly believe Mike's story, but Mike's gentle nature would not allow him to be anything but courteous. Walking out into the Mexican sun, Mike recalled the man's aloof tone and thought, *We all know what that kind of brushoff means . . . "Don't call us. We'll call you."*

Ravenous and weary, Mike met Alan and Phillip at the coffee house. They ate a sandwich while Mike filled them in on his visit. Sipping a cup of hot coffee, Alan began, "I told you I should have gone with you. I have connections. They would have listened to me," he continued.

"Whatever," Mike thought as he rolled his eyes. "Let's go back to the hotel and catch a nap," Alan suggested.

"Sounds good to me," Mike said. "My head is killing me."

The small hotel had simply served as a place to lay their heads at night and was in no way elaborate. It was, however, centrally located and had air-conditioning—the only two prerequisites in finding a place to stay. The guys entered their rooms. Mike quickly noticed that his clothes and belongings were in disarray. Clothes were strewn all over the floor.

"What's up?" he wondered. He knocked on the connecting door. Alan and Phillip's clothes had been scattered all over the floor, too. Alan's paranoia had thankfully made him mark the room. On leaving for the day, Alan placed a match in the doorframe. On returning Alan noticed the match lying on the floor in front of his door before he entered his room.

Someone had been in the rooms, but who? "Quick, gather your stuff. We're getting outta here," Alan commanded in a whisper. They gathered their belongings and began walking down the hallway.

"Wait," Alan said. "Someone's coming. Let's go down the back stairs.

God's hand is sovereign. Fifty police officers stormed through the lobby and up the hallway to the rooms where the men had just left. Something Alan said while in the police station must have thrown suspicion on them. *What did Alan say to warrant this kind of suspicion?* Mike wondered. They ran down the back stairs and hoped to reach safety. One can only imagine what might have happened if Mike had been thrown into a Mexican jail. I've heard horror stories about this very thing. Needless to say, the men did not stop. They ran to the big red truck and left town! The exhausted travelers returned to Bacalar late the next day.

While Mike and the guys were gone, I had my first real confrontation with the devil. Because of a lack of sleep and nourishment, my mind began playing tricks on me. My faith was wearing thin. I was blaming much of this whole ordeal on myself. Playing the blame game can take you far from the truth, but you are unaware of just how misconstrued your thoughts can become. I began rethinking all the bad decisions we made leading up to Brittany's disappearance. They were numerous. I believed that everything had been my fault.

Feeling low and desperate, I made my way up to the third story of the house. As I stood on the roof, I looked over the

edge and wondered, *If I jump, is it high enough to kill me?*
Thoughts of jumping over the side and falling to my death
took over my psyche. I stood on top of the house sobbing and
wondering whether if I jumped, Brittany would return. *If I
died, would she return home?* I wondered. *If the fall only
injured me, would she return home then?*

As I stood staring over the edge, my eyes filled with tears.
Will God forgive me if I commit suicide? I thought. *I can't hide
this from God.* I stood trembling. *But where is God?* I asked
myself. I had not felt Him in days. *Even He has abandoned
me,* I thought. And I didn't blame Him one bit! But I was a
coward. I could not jump—not today.

Trembling, I stood in the heat and decided not to jump.
The whole experience seemed surreal, as though I was not in
my own body but somewhere far away watching. Trying to
make sense of the pain and dejection, I stood in a trancelike
state. From the recesses of my mind I heard a noise. A ringing.
The phone was ringing. But I was not sleeping . . ..

Wait, I thought. *The phone is ringing, or is it?* I questioned
myself. *Yes,* I thought, *it's really ringing.* I frantically ran down
the stairs as fast as I could.

"Hello," I said.

"Mom, are you OK?" It was Chris. "Mom, is something
wrong?" he asked again.

"Oh, my gosh," I thought. My knees crumbled under me.
Falling to the floor, I thought, *I almost jumped. I would never
have seen Chris again. Thank you, God, for making me a coward today.*

I felt ashamed. Moments earlier I questioned whether God
was still with me. Being the faithful Father, He showed up.

"Hey, son," I said as I tried to pull myself together. "I'm
fine. Just lonely! You're dad is gone to Mexico City again."

"Well, Mom, my flight leaves the day after tomorrow from Jackson at 5:30 a.m. and arrives in Cancun at 2:30 p.m. Will Dad be home so ya'll can pick me up?" he asked.

"Yeah, I think so," I said. We talked for a few minutes about the fax and the article. He, too, was puzzled.

"Mom, it makes no sense, but I'm flying down there. I'm going to find her. I'm not leaving until I do," he said with resolve. How great to hear his precious voice! Oh, how I loved him for calling at that very moment!

"Thank You, God," I whispered once again. He did seem to rescue me often.

I hung up the phone, sat on the floor, and wept. God had not abandoned me, He was right there. I could not see Him because I was wallowing in self-pity and pain.

Chapter 14

Beauty Among the Ashes

Mental exhaustion wore on Mike and me. But Chris's arrival brought new hope—a fresh pair of eyes to see things in a different light. When Mike and I arrived at the Cancun airport, Chris' plane had just landed. Minutes passed. Then I saw Chris walking toward us. He had a huge smile on his face. His blue eyes twinkled like lights on a Christmas tree. His beautiful white teeth sparkled as he walked toward us. A surge of new life ran through my veins. For the first time in weeks I felt alive. I ran toward him. Chris opened his arms wide. I jumped into them. His sparkling eyes met mine.

My son, I thought. *My beautiful son!* He picked me up and twirled me around as he kissed my cheek.

"I'm here, Mom," he said. My eyes began to well up with tears. I felt safe again. I felt good to be in his arms. I loved to smell his hair and look into his crystal-clear eyes.

Chris could help us work through this nightmare, or so I thought. On the way home, Chris told us that he had emailed Brittany.

"Dad," he began. "I wrote Brittany and told her that I was traveling to Mexico City to visit a buddy of mine. I asked her if we could meet up and talk WITH NO PARENTS, MOM!" Chris glanced at me and waited for my reaction. But anger had long left my spirit.

"OK, Chris, whatever works," I said.

As we drove back to Bacalar, we sorted through all the information we had so far. Mike told Chris about his activities in Mexico City with Alan and Phillip. Chris was not totally convinced that these two characters were who they said they were. "Dad, are you sure they can help?" Chris inquired.

"I don't know, Chris," Mike said. "They have been enthusiastic. Besides, we don't have anyone else. They're all we have right now," he continued.

Without Mike and me knowing, Pastor Randy and Chris had been talking about our situation. Once home Chris told us about the arsenal of people who were helping us in the Plano and Dallas area. "Mom, Pastor Randy collected money for the search. One couple in the church gave $10,000 for the effort!" Chris said.

"What? Oh, my gosh! That's amazing," I said. I was overwhelmed. *How could someone care so much about our plight?* I thought. My sister, Lauren, contacted FOX 4 News on running a story. The TV station interviewed Lauren and Pastor Randy. Hundreds of dollars had been donated. So many calls flooded the church switchboard, they had to hire another receptionist because of the high volume of people calling with prayers and donations. Lauren spent countless hours visiting with a variety of reporters at the TV station. Humbled beyond belief, I called my beautiful sister. Her loyalty meant more than words could ever say. Then I called our wonderful pastor to thank him for all his efforts.

Another meeting of the minds was in order. Alan, Phillip, Mike, and Chris combed the emails for some kind of clue. Sizing up Alan and Phillip took Chris about five minutes, but for once he agreed with us. They were all we had!

Chris checked his email account to see if Brittany replied. "Mom, I have an email from Brittany!" Chris exclaimed. The whole group hovered around the tiny computer screen to read the desired email.

Chris:

I am fine. I don't want to meet with you right now.
I know mom and dad are looking for me. They said
bad things about Aldo. I could be a
prostitute. I could be an exotic dancer. Maybe,
maybe not. Tell them to stop looking for me.
It is my life and I don't want to live with them any
more. Thank you for wanting to meet with me, but I can't
trust you.

Hugs and kisses,
Brittany

No one quite knew how to react to what we just read. Chris was hurt. Mike and I were dumfounded. "Is she telling us that she's a prostitute?" I asked with horror in my voice.

Dejected, Mike sat on the sofa and placed his face in his calloused hands. Even his strength was waning. "What do we do now?" Mike asked in a whisper. "She's my daughter. Why can't she understand that I won't give up until we see for ourselves that she's alive? If she would just meet with us to show us she's all right," he continued.

Chris sat on the army cot and held a pillow tight to his chest. As he thought about the email, he said, "Why in the world would she not trust me? We are so tight. We talk about stuff all the time. She knows she can trust me. What's she thinking?" Hurt and confused, Chris walked into the kitchen and sat at the table. He wanted to be alone.

Mike and I had almost become accustomed to these puzzling emails full of rejection and disdain. But Chris was another matter altogether. He grew up knowing that his sister idolized him. He knew with great certainty that she would do anything he asked of her. Well, evidently someone else possessed a power over Brittany greater than her undying loyalty for her brother. He was angry with Brittany for even considering not trusting him.

Disgusted at this latest weird email, Mike sat down at the computer and began to write her yet another request.

Dear Brittany:

We love you! If you want to show us that you are OK, then meet with us. Let's talk. If you don't want to come home, that's OK. Just meet with us and show us you're alive. If you don't meet with us, then we'll keep looking for you FOREVER! We have to know you're OK! Do you need money? I can send you some. We love you!!!!

Love,
Dad

"She has to have some feeling for us. She has to care about us, Vanda. We have to try," Mike said. "If we can get her to pick up money from Western Union, then we can use the tracking number to see where she picked it up," Mike said with excitement in his voice.

"Now that's a good idea, Mike," I said. I wondered whether this would ever end.

While we were working through the newest wave of pain and rejection, Phillip was working on the IP address of this latest email. After about three hours Phillip said, "I got it. The email came from another location in Mexico City.

"Wait, Vanda," Mike said. "Check your email and see if she sent you a message." My mailbox was empty. No luck!

Phillip began looking for a pattern in the IP addresses. He located a map of Mexico City's different zones. Several emails had been sent from the same place.

The letter Ernestina received was sent from a business close to the place where the first emails were sent. This new email was sent from a different IP address, but it appeared to be in close proximity to the others.

Alan finished his cigarette and said, "I think we should return to Mexico City. We should check into a hotel close to where these emails are being sent and wait for her to send another one. Mike, you email her and tell her that you're going to send her $100. But you're not going to send it."

"Why not?" Mike inquired. "That way she'll email again. By then, we'll be in Mexico City. Just maybe we'll be able to catch her at the Internet store.

"Vanda, if she calls you, tell her that Mike had trouble sending the money because he needs a location to send it to," Alan continued.

"OK, now you're thinking," Mike said.

"This sounds like it might actually work," Chris said. Excitement filled the house once again.

Not again. They're not leaving again? I wondered. But I remained silent. I didn't want to thwart any possibility of finding her, no matter what I was going through when left here alone. I waited in silence. The men talked for a while.

Finally, Mike said, "OK, one more trip. That's it. If we don't spot her, we're returning immediately."

"Chris," I began with my heart pounding. "Do you want to stay here with me?"

He looked at me with surprise and said, "Mom, I flew all the way down here to find Brittany. I'm going."

"OK," I said fearfully. I wasn't sure I could deal with another trip and more isolation. But I kept my fears to myself.

The guys gathered their stuff and were off by 8:30 p.m. Maybe Chris would be the right addition we needed to turn things around. Alone again. I loaded *Anna and the King* into the VCR again. What a beautiful love story! I had memorized it, but I still cried at the ending. I prayed, "Please, God. Let them find her. Oh, Father, please. I don't know how much more of this I can take."

I walked up the stairs to lie down. Lying on the bed, I listened to the waves lapping gently against the dock. The fan whirled as I closed my eyes and tried to calm my soul. Sleep was long in arriving. It did not last long before the dream encroached on my psyche. The phone was ringing. I woke up and ran down the stairs in the darkness to the phone. As I picked it up, the droning dial tone loudly reverberated through the receiver. No one was there.

Miserable and alone, I walked slowly back to my bed, only to stare at the ceiling and wait for sleep to return. I prayed, "Please, Father, take this dream from me. It's eating away at my mind, Father. I can't stand it. I need to sleep, please," I begged. Somewhere in the darkness, I dozed off into a peaceful slumber.

The sun peeped over the lake at 5 a.m. Sunlight filled my room. I slowly rose. Coffee and a cold shower sounded good. I caught a glimpse of my naked body in the mirror. *I'm wasting away*, I said to myself in dismay. It was the first time in days I had looked in the mirror. My haggard face bore dark circles under my eyes. *I have to get some sleep*, I said as I looked back at my reflection. *And I have to eat something*, I thought. I went downstairs and made coffee and toast while I played countless games of Solitaire. Alone and isolated from the world, this silly game of Solitaire gave me some comfort. I could play, then push the button, and new game would appear.

This mindless repetition would drone on for hours. Before I knew it, noon arrived. Time for an exciting lunch of ham and cheese and then to my chair outside, where I read a Christian novel and let warm rays embrace my body. Hours whiled away before the phone rang.

"Hello," I said.

"Mom, it's me." Chris began. "We just arrived at the hotel. We're going to the Internet store where the last email was sent. Dad will call tonight and give you an update," Chris said with love in his voice. "Mom, are you OK?"

With a half-forced smile, "Yeah, I'm good," I said. "Just miss you guys. I wish I were there with you. I'll be fine. Thanks for calling. I love you, Chris." Several hours passed before I decided to make myself something to eat. I had macaroni and *creama* and watched another movie. Day two droned into day three.

The next day as I sat outside in the sun, the phone rang. "Hello," my heart beat rapidly as I spoke with anticipation.

"Mom, it's me. I got your email, and yes, I could use some money."

It was Brittany! "OK, honey, I said. "Just tell me where to send it. Dad will be off to Chetumal."

"Just tell him to send it to Mexico City," she said.

"We need to know the name of a place that is close to you, Brittany. Western Union needs an area where the money will be sent to," I stated.

"OK, forget it then. Bye." The phone went dead.

MAN! I blew it! I said to myself. Before I returned to my chair, I tried to call Mike. No service rang through the receiver in Spanish. An hour passed before the phone rang again.

"Mom, OK, send the money," Brittany said. "Send it to the Central Mexican Bank in Zona Central," she said with anger in her voice.

Her anger puzzled me. "Shouldn't we be the ones angry?" I wondered.

"OK, we will. Are you OK, Brittany?" I asked. She hung up the phone before she could answer.

I quickly picked up the phone and said a quick prayer. "Please, Father, let me get through this time."

It rang. "Hello?" Mike answered. I gave him the news. He looked on the map and located the bank Brittany mentioned. "Vanda, now all we have to do is wait for her to pick up the money." Or so we thought! Phillip and Chris staked out the bank at a juice bar from across the street. Hours passed. The bank closed. Brittany had not surfaced.

Mike and Alan were sitting across from the Internet café. The guys spoke with the owner. He recalled seeing Aldo and Brittany a few days before. They were hopeful she would return. No luck! She had not surfaced at either place.

The next morning Alan and Mike went to Western Union to check on the money. It had been picked up. She had picked it up at a bank five miles from where they were. So close and yet so far . . ..

Mike and Chris decided to visit the bank and talk to the manager. They entered the bank—the same bank Brittany visited the day before. Chris used his charm and pleaded with the manager to see the tape.

After much supplication, the manager finally agreed to let them view the video. *Wait! She was on the tape.* She appeared fine. Aldo was right beside her. He did not have a tight hold on her as if he were forcing her to do anything she didn't want to do. She signed for the money and was out of the bank in less than five minutes. The guys knew they were close, so they stayed a few days and walked around. They watched the Internet café and showed Brittany's picture to hundreds of people but had no luck.

As evening approached on the fourth day, a man on the street recognized Brittany. "Yes, I've seen her," the stranger said. He then was shown pictures of Alejandra and Aldo. "Yes, she's with them," he continued. I've seen them around for the past week or so."

"They must be staying at a hotel around here, Dad," Chris said. Encouraged, they searched every hotel, business, and restaurant in the area. But the trio appeared to have vanished off the face of the earth!

While Mike, Chris, and the two cartoon characters were off playing detective, I was sinking once again into the great abyss of lies and deceit. The devil decided to reappear and work his black magic on me once again. I now know how men in the brig feel after days of isolation. An evil force continued to draw me up to the rooftop. I returned once again up to the third story of the house. Sleep had evaded my soul for weeks on end. My mind played wild tricks on me! I stood on the roof and looked at the emerald green grass. I stared over the edge for a long while.

Trembling with fear, I began to pray. "God, I can't do it! I can't stand it any more. I'm sorry. I'm not strong! Mike's strong—not me! Forgive me, Father, but I can't do it any more. She'll return home if I'm dead! I know she will!" *But what if the fall doesn't kill me?* I wondered with blurry vision as the tears filled my eyes.

Standing over the edge, my heart pounded as I uttered, "It's OK. My broken, mangled body will eventually give up, and death will take my pain away. She never liked me telling her what to do, and she always resented me for trying to protect her. Mike and Chris will be better off without me, too."

With my eyes filled with tears, I looked over the edge and readied myself to jump. I was too broken to help anyone at this point, least of all, myself. This was the only option left for me. My mind was so warped from no sleep or nourishment that I believed I was actually thinking rationally.

With one last breath, I prayed. "God, if you are here, and if you love me, send me a sign. If you have something more for me, send me a sign." I stood waiting and looking over the edge of the high, white wall . . ..

In an instant, a white butterfly appeared . . . then two . . . and then three . . . and four. They were flying all around me. White butterflies began to appear out of nowhere. I wept and trembled. My knees grew weak. In another moment at least a dozen white butterflies surrounded my space.

Trembling and in a state of bewilderment, I lifted my hand toward one of the beautiful white butterflies swirling around me. The white symbol of hope fluttered close to my palm and flew just out of my grasp. My heart fluttered in synchronicity with its wings. These exquisite insects did not fly too far from my reach until they sensed I was certain they were from God. My whole body quivered. Soon I felt a comforting spirit envelop me. The Holy Spirit wrapped His comforting arms around me. Fear left. I felt Satan's evil demon flee my spirit.

Filled with peace, I fell into a heap on the rough cement floor and began sobbing. *Wow! What just happened?* I questioned. *Amazing!*

Moments passed as my heart tried to recover. I managed to whimper through soft tears. *Was it real?* I wondered to myself. With my heart beating wildly and my body quivering, I said, "Yes." I had just experienced my own miracle from God! God did love me! He had not abandoned me. He was there, right beside me. He rescued me in my darkest moment! I felt so humbled that God cared for me. It truly was a miraculous visitation from my Father.

Broken and exhausted, my trembling legs walked down stairs. Quivering like a young calf, I managed to make my way into the den. I fell on the army green sofa with my last ounce of strength. Fear dissipated from my soul. Fatigued, I laid my head down and began to fall into a dreamless sleep. Hours passed before I woke from my peaceful slumber. The house was dark, but as I sat on the sofa, I felt no angst—only peace.

Sitting on the cot, I replayed my experience over again in my head. *Was that God?* I wondered again with my doubting psyche. My spirit said, "Yes." But my mind began to question the whole incident. "Man, God's presence was so powerful," I said as I sat in the darkness of the room. I began to think about Moses and how even he was unable to behold the glory of God.

Amazed at God's awesomeness, I curled up into a fetal position. For the first time in a long while, I felt safe.

During the past several years this memory has fluttered back to visit me. Each time I replay that moment in my head, I'm amazed at God's sovereign hand. He knew that I reached my breaking point. He knew I was going to jump to my death. He knew me. He knew!

On numerous occasions I have seen my butterflies. I realize that by themselves, these butterflies are not rare nor special but are in fact very ordinary, just like me. However, all I have to do it seems is to call out to God and ask Him to flutter by. Within seconds, one or two beautiful white butterflies appear out of nowhere.

One day last February, I sat on my back patio and pondered whether God could be glorified by my memoir. Within seconds four white butterflies danced for me. They materialized out of thin air and flapped their delicate, lacy transparent wings. I felt God say "Yes!"

Since that incident I have seen numerous white butterflies fly just for me. All I have to do as I am driving down the street is call out to God and ask Him to flutter by. He does.

During the past year I have tried to count the number of times God has appeared to me with His fluttering wings, but this has become an impossible task. As I share my encounter with others, they say, "I have never seen a white butterfly. Where do they come from?"

I respond, "They are from God. Each one special and unique, just as our Father's children are special and unique."

Sometimes we have no words to describe God's sovereign hand.

Chapter 15

The Devil in Designer Clothes

On their return, Mike and the guys grew discouraged at their lack of progress. Everyone's patience was wearing thin. We started looking for somewhere to lay the blame. Chris possessed a superhero complex of sorts. His idealistic young ego believed that he would simply travel down to Mexico and find Brittany! If only things were that easy . . ..

March 15, 2001. Tempers began to flare from months of stress and frustration. Tension filled the air. For some reason Mike looked at me and said. "It's your fault she's gone. You don't pray enough. You don't spend enough time with God."

"What? Where in the world did that come from?" I began. "Are you suggesting that my relationship with God, or lack thereof, is the cause of all this?" Crushed, I looked into Mike's eyes and for the first time could see anger—anger toward me.

My flesh and pride broke through. I was angered. I yelled at Mike, my soulmate. "How could you question my faith and relationship with God?" I asked with disdain in my voice.

When you give the devil an in, boy, he takes it and runs with it! I was on the brink of exploding at Mike with both barrels loaded. *Wait,* I thought. *I'm not doing this!* I said as I walked away hurt by Mike's stinging words. I felt guilty enough without his pointing out my failures. *Not today*, I thought as walked around the corner to hide in the kitchen.

Chris walked around the corner and dropped another bomb! "Mom, I don't see how you can't HATE GOD for doing this to you. You guys sold everything you owned to move down here in this godforsaken place! Look what He did.

He didn't protect you; He let it happen!" My eyes bugged out of my head with complete surprise. Chris continued to question our circumstance, "Dad, how could God let this happen to you guys? You don't deserve this."

My mind had careened through all of these ideas before, but now the three of us were at odds with each other at a time in which we should be standing together. Even though I had not shared with my family my miracle of the butterflies, I knew God had not forsaken us. Moreover, I felt His gentle hand guiding us through rough waters. I knew my words would give little comfort to Chris. He was hurting. Questions and rejection filled his spirit. He did not understand any of this. And to top it off, his sister rejected him. He was hurt beyond belief, even though he never said as much. Chris is a man of few words. But I had to try and find some words to comfort my son.

Searching my soul for something profound to say, I myself began to wonder why this happened to our family. But with love I began, "God didn't do this, Chris," I said in a voice filled with sorrow. "Yes, He let it happen," I whispered. "And why, I don't know. I don't think we'll ever know why certain things happen. But He didn't do this. I know you're frustrated with us, with Brittany, with the whole thing, and we are, too. We have to find a way to get through this together," I said. I was trying to convince myself as much as I was him. Shutting down, I walked outside and began mumbling to myself.

Chris was reared in the church, but he didn't share many of our beliefs. In fact, in college he began to question the mere existence of God. As Mike and I grew closer to the Lord, over time Chris' heart seemed to grow cold toward God and religion in general.

Brittany had been missing for about 70 days. Our pastor, our friends, and our family begged us to move back to Texas where we could at least lean on our support group for strength. But Mike and I had made a promise not to leave Mexico until we found her! Dozens of prayers flooded my email account on a daily basis. Some of the prayers were from as far away as China and Japan. Mike and I believed we had to stay. Brittany was only 15; we couldn't leave her in a foreign country!

As the sun set, Mike called me in from the dock. We needed to support each other rather than tear each other apart. Apologies were made by all and to all. We needed to get the creative juices flowing and formulate another plan. But I was brain dead. My spirit was crushed; I was shutting down. Mike's words reverberated through my head. *How long has he been thinking that I am the cause of the whole ordeal?* I wondered. "You don't pray enough" through my head over and over despite the fact that I commanded these words to leave in Jesus' name!

Tension filled the air, but we all managed to be civil to each other. Too many hurtful words had already been said. We had no need to exacerbate the situation any further. We decided to check my email before we went to bed. Whenever we were stumped, we checked our email to see if she had contacted us. I logged in. I had mail. Click. Wow! "Mike, Chris, I have an email from Brittany," I said with hope in my voice.

Chris was lying on the army cot with one leg crossed over the other. "What's it say, Mom?" he inquired. Mike stood looking over my shoulder. The email read:

Dear Mom & Dad:

Stop looking for me! I will not meet with you.
I am watched all the time, maybe by the police.

Important people are looking out for me.
People are protecting me. I am not with them
any more. I will not meet with Chris. I am fine.

Love,
Brittany

Every email appeared to be some kind of an enigma—a riddle we were supposed to be able to solve. I had no idea what message she was trying to send. "What does Brittany mean she's being watched by the police?" I asked. "Maybe she's a prostitute, maybe she's being watched by the police, people are protecting her . . .. What the heck does all this mean?" I asked with frustration.

Chris walked over to the computer screen, "Move, Mom," he said. "Let me look at it."

"Dad," Chris began. "What was the IP address from the other emails?" he asked.

Mike retrieved them; they began comparing the addresses against each other. "This new one matches the first few emails. Do you think they move often or just visit different Internet cafés?" Chris asked.

No one had any answers. I was constantly amazed that while I ran on my emotions, Mike and Chris mainly dealt through this ordeal with a methodical logic. Here I was analyzing the stupid email and wondering what it all meant. And Mike and Chris just begin dissecting it. As I sat and watched them both sitting around the computer, a tinge of jealousy crept into my spirit.

Mike's frustration and feelings of powerlessness mounted. As he paced around the room, he began, "I want to go back to Mexico City. No goons, just Chris and me. I want to go visit the American Consulate without Alan and Phillip hanging over my shoulder messing things up. I feel so powerless. I hate Aldo for this!" he said with great resolve. Moving toward me he whispered, "I'm sorry for what I said earlier. I'm just so frustrated and hurt. She's my girl. I can't rest until someone listens to me. Someone has to care enough to help us." His precious hands touched mine. He pulled me into him and held me close. Mike began to weep softly and said, "Vanda, forgive me please."

"I already have," I said. "This nightmare is closing in on us. We have to remain sane somehow. I love you, Mike."

If only I could close my eyes and it would disappear . . .. Mike believed he had to try to get through to the consulate one more time. "Vanda," he began. "I feel like I have to visit with Mr. Ramirez again. I know he wasn't very hospitable before, but I just can't rest until I talk with him again."

"OK, Mike," I said. "Whatever you think is best." Before they left, Mike and Chris gathered the emails, the magazine, the fax, and clothes. I dreaded being left alone again, but I knew my butterflies would protect me from harm. I would be all right.

I woke up early only to hear the phone ring. "Who could that be?" I questioned as I ran down the stairs.

"Hello," I said.

"Hey, Vanda! Can I come over?" Wendy asked.

"Yeah, sure, what's up?" I asked.

"I'll tell you when I get there," she said and hung up.

Wendy moved to Bacalar in 1995. She quit her stressful job in Florida, sold most of her belongings, and moved to our little community. To earn a living she drove an ambulance in Chetumal four days a week and ran a laundry service out of her house. She did most of our laundry. Thank God. Wendy was somewhat stuck in the 1970s: flower power, long hair, bell-bottoms, dangerous men, and a little weed.

A knock at the door a few minutes later ushered Wendy into the house. Flustered and excited she began, "Vanda, I have some news for you. My boyfriend hangs around some pretty shady guys. They were talking the other night about making a porn movie. The star of the movie is going to be a young American girl. Rumor has it they are flying the girl in from Mexico City."

Shock and terror ran through my veins. "Do you think they mean Brittany?" I asked. "Where? When? How?" I asked. My mind was reeling out of control. *How can this be happening?* I wondered. A few moments went by in silence.

"Where's Mike?" Wendy asked.

"He's in Mexico City again," I said. "Wendy," I began. "Mike's not here." I thought for a moment. "Do you think you can take me to Alan's house?" I asked. "Maybe he can help. I knew he usually messed things up, but I had no other option.

On the way to Alan's house, Wendy filled me in on what she knew about the scheme. American businessmen were fronting the money for the X-rated movie. They were shooting in a seaside village, Mahahual, a remote village located an hour from Bacalar. Evidently large sums of money exchanged hands in order to secure the American actress.

"Please, God, don't let it be Brittany," I pleaded in a quiet voice. Once again I felt as if I were on a ride at a carnival. I felt as if I might faint. My stomach was tied in knots; my head reeled with ideas and possible scenarios as to Brittany's fate if she was actually the American actress.

Alan's small house sat in a large hole. The ill-kempt house appeared to have been painted about 10 years earlier. Cobwebs hung down from the cinderblock structure. As I exited Wendy's truck, I yelled, *"Buenos.* Hello, anybody there?"

Alan stepped through the door and was smoking a cigarette. "Yeah, who's there? What'd you want?" he asked.

"Alan, it's me, Vanda. Can I talk with you, please?" I asked. He motioned me into his yard. Wendy stayed in the truck. We stood outside in the steamy heat. I told him of our new dilemma. Wheels began turning in his brain. He was devising a plan. His eyes lit up.

A hush fell over us as Alan's brain began to tick with possibilities. After several minutes of heat-sweltering silence, his eyes grew large. An eerie smile appeared. "I think I'll pay these gentlemen a little visit," he said with wild eyes. Since he had been in the CIA, he owned several unregistered guns and was not afraid to use them. "I have an idea," he said. "I have two bottles of tequila. Phillip and I will go to their house tonight. We'll play cards, get them drunk, and find out what they know," he said with a crazy stare. "I'll get it outta them, don't you worry."

Worry? Now I was really worried about what these guys were going to do. He continued, "I've got ways of finding out anything." I couldn't believe what I was hearing, but I was desperate.

"OK, whatever it takes," I said. Petrified at the idea of him possibly beating the men up, I was shocked that Alan would arrive at this conclusion so quickly. But the fact that I would go along with such an outlandish plan scared me even more. I was turning into a desperate woman: a woman driven by fear and an insatiable desire to find her daughter.

Nervous and wondering if the whole thing would blow up in our faces, I didn't sleep much at all that night. It was 2:30 a.m. The phone rang. It was Alan.

"Vanda, hide quick! Things got a little outta hand tonight. There was a fight. Phillip and I were followed. We lost 'em, but they know I've been working for you and Mike. One of them owns a boat. They may be coming to your house to take out their revenge on you."

"Oh, great, Alan," I screamed. "I'm here alone. Where am I supposed to go?"

"Well, maybe they won't find you" he said.

Oh, my gosh, I thought. *What an idiot I am for going to him in the first place.*

"Be careful. I'll see you tomorrow," Alan said. Before he hung up the phone, he added, "Oh, good news. Brittany's not the girl in the movie!"

Hanging up the phone, I questioned, *Oh, great. What did he do? What could've happened?*

Panic and apprehension filled me. I sat downstairs cuddling my thin, brown legs up into my chest on the sofa and waited for the sound of a boat. Terrified, I wondered, *What am I going to do to if someone attempts to break into the house?* Hours ticked by. No boat! No danger but fear nonetheless filled me. *What a way to live*, I thought. Morning was almost here. I tried to call Mike. No service reverberated through the receiver — again.

The early morning sun rose over the beautiful crystal water. The phone rang and awakened me from a drowsy sleep. It was Mike. Thank God. I replayed the previous day's events and told him about the X-rated movie in Mahahual, Alan's encounter with the men, and the threat on my life. This sounded like something out of a crime novel.

Mike had news of his own. He and Chris visited the American Embassy, but the visit did not go well. Mike began, "Mr. Ramirez was very courteous, but his patience seemed to be wearing a bit thin. Vanda, he told me that he had been in contact with the State Department and that they are now aware of the situation."

"Mike, that's great, isn't it?" I asked.

I heard an awkward silence on the other end of the phone. "Mike, are you still there?" I asked.

"Yeah, I'm trying to figure out how to tell you what happened next," he said in a near whisper.

"Just say it," I said.

"The director asked Chris what he thought, Vanda. Chris told Mr. Ramirez that he thought she ran away," he said with hesitation.

"WHAT?" I yelled. "How could Chris say that? Doesn't he know how important it is for us to be unified?" I loved Chris so much, but this really hurt us. We had no proof that she ran away. Why would she run away with a 45-year-old man? But the idea had been introduced. We could not turn back. Now we would have to fight both the news article and the idea that she left on her own.

Mike felt my frustration. "Vanda, we're coming home. We have nothing left for us to do here."

Mike and Chris returned home with no leads or new information. Another dead end—each one seemed to bring more heartache. The three of us had no idea what to do next. I was angry with Chris. I asked him what made him think Brittany went with them voluntarily. "Mom, think about it. Why would she want to live here? She hates school. She wants to be an adult. It makes sense that she would leave with them," he said coldly.

My heart and my mind couldn't accept any of those reasons for a daughter's lies and deception. So we agreed to disagree. Chris in his stubbornness nonetheless decided to stay and help us find her. Our precious son put his life on hold to help in our search. He put his job in jeopardy. The construction crew where he worked building log homes needed him in Jackson. He abandoned it all for us. Chris was our amazing strong tower in the midst of hell.

Chapter 16

False Prophets

After several days in which we had no leads or sense of direction, Pastor Randy called. He had learned about a group of private investigators who find missing children of missionary families. Pastor Randy, concerned that Brittany might have run away, asked the agency if it would still find her even if that were the case. The people there assured us that they would find her no matter what. Several days passed before we heard a knock at the door. Steve and David stood in the doorway with backpacks and equipment in hand. Now all we had to do was to find a way to get rid of Alan and Phillip, the two hoodlums from cartoonland.

Steve and David seemed competent and well-trained. Steve and David stayed at a hotel in town. The hotel had musty, prison-type mattresses, a shower that trickled cold water, and bugs that littered the floor. We all spent the first day of their arrival reliving everything that had happened during the past 85 days. We went through every email, phone conversation, the fax, the magazine article, the guys' multiple visits to Mexico City—everything. All that was left to do was to search Brittany's room, again.

David and Steve went through every inch of her room and looked for clues. Not much was there, but we did find a calendar on which Brittany had made several notations about different days' events. On January 6 she had written, "Go to Chetumal with Alejandra." A smiley face was on the square next to the message. I looked at it and wondered, *What in the world could that mean?*

A tracking device was placed on the phone. In most places in the world it would identify the origin of the call, but we would soon learn that the device must have worked everywhere except Mexico. They also installed a phone recorder that we used to record Brittany's calls. Now all we had to do was wait.

We didn't have to wait long. Brittany phoned that afternoon. As the phone rang, the device registered an unknown number. Maybe it was from Brittany. It was.

Steve pushed the record button. Mike began talking to Brittany.

"Hello," he said.

"Dad, it's me," Brittany said.

"Hey, girl," Mike said in a tender voice. "What'cha doing?"

"I was wondering if you could send me some more money," Brittany said.

"Well, I don't know, Brittany," Mike began. "How much do you need?"

"About $500. I need to get some things."

"Well, we don't have that much, but we could send you $100. Will that do?" he asked.

"Yeah, I guess so," Brittany answered with disappointment in her voice.

"OK, then, where shall I send it?" Mike asked.

"Mexico City," she continued.

As I mentioned before, Western Union is careful about sending money. It asks that you send money to a specific location. "Brittany," Mike began again. "I need something more specific than that. Can you give me an area, please?"

"Send it to the Central zone," she said.

"OK, I'll send it tomorrow," Mike said. "Do you want to talk to your mom?" he asked, but Brittany hung up the phone.

Mike looked at me and saw the hurt in my hazel eyes. With each passing day Brittany appeared to be moving further away. Today the knife dug a little deeper. She refused to talk to me.

Putting my personal feelings aside, I clasped my hands and asked David, "Do you think the recorder worked?"

Steve rewound the tape. We listened to the conversation. "Listen for background noise," David said. Maybe it will give us a clue as to her whereabouts. We listened to the tape. We listened again. Cars raced by; people talked in the background, but we couldn't make out whose voices we heard.

"Her voice doesn't sound as if she is under duress," Steve said. "Her voice pattern is even. She appears to be fine.

"She sounds fine, but is she fine?" Mike asked. "We don't know if she's OK or not!"

The phone identification device listed a number. After extensive research, the number was found to be a pay phone somewhere in Mexico City. What a surprise! I had to hand it to Aldo. If you don't want to be found, go to the biggest and busiest city in the world—and the most corrupt city as well.

Mike went into Chetumal and sent the money. We waited for her to pick it up. With the tracking number, we were able to check the website any time day or night. We thought that would turn out to be a good thing, but she never picked up the money. Two days passed; she still hadn't retrieved the money. *Why had she asked for the money in the first place if she wasn't going to get it?* I wondered. Again, no answers; the unanswered questions seemed to be piling up. They baffled our minds and continued to drive us insane.

Our new knights in shining armor, David and Steve, stayed a total of four days. Then they were gone. They assured us that they would stay in touch. They were only a phone call away. Once the men returned to California, they put a report together for Pastor Randy. They concluded that Brittany ran away. She was able to return home any time she wanted. The report stated that because she was able to call home and email us, she was in no real danger. They spoke to Pastor Randy over the phone. Their investigation was complete. They would search for her no longer. This puzzled us all.

We believed we had no real evidence that she was *not* in danger. The men had also previously stated that they would find her no matter the circumstances of her disappearance. But they reneged on their part of the bargain and considered the case closed. Now we had been lied to again—this time by a missionary agency. *Can no one keep his word?* I wondered with a heavy sigh and heavy heart.

"How did they arrive at that conclusion?" Mike asked as he shook his head in disgust.

"I don't know, Mike. I just wish this whole thing wasn't so confusing." I said. We were back to square one, which was nowhere but a big empty desert of puzzlement.

Pastor Randy considered Chris to be the most objective member of our family in light of all the information gathered. The church elders wanted to have a meeting to go over any remaining options that might be available, so they flew Chris back to Plano for a meeting. FOX 4 News had interviewed Pastor Randy and my sister, Lauren, for the third time. Donations and inquiry calls were still bombarding the church on a daily basis. The congregation desired to be informed as well. Many people cared about Brittany's well being, but still no one could find her.

During all of this, my mom was still busy trying to find someone—anyone—to listen. Her persistence finally paid off. José Guerrmo from the National Center for Missing and Exploited Children in Washington D.C. wanted to help. Hooray! A fresh lead! If I learned anything through all of this, it is to persevere no matter what. Our minds and our bodies were weary. We wanted to give up. But an undying love for our daughter and the fear that she was in danger kept us looking for her. Besides, I had made Aldo a promise. I would search for her forever. I was beginning to feel as though I had already searched forever.

After making contact, emailing back and forth, and several phone conversations, Guerrmo believed I should make a trip to Washington, D.C. and speak with him in person. Arrangements were made. Mom and Dad were to meet me in D.C. and stand beside me. Boy, was I glad they were going to be there for mental and spiritual support! My mom's persistence paid off. She used her Southern charm to set up a meeting with an agent of the FBI and with someone in the State Department. My steel magnolia was on my side. I was so grateful!

On April 5, 2001, I boarded a plane. Brittany had disappeared almost 90 days ago. We knew that with each passing day she slipped further and further from our grasp and our influence. We knew that the influence of Abel Martine Lopez Rodriguez, also known as Aldo, was growing daily.

Once I was in Washington, D.C., José Guerrmo along with several staff members who worked at the National Center for Missing and Exploited Children met with me. One woman took copious notes and asked questions. The *TV Notas* magazine was passed around. Questions were asked and answered. Honesty was something I thought would be rewarded. I did not hold anything back from them. I was forthright about every secret or possibility.

After several hours of briefing them on the situation and a variety of questions on their end, they gave me the sad news. They could not help me because the child had not been taken on U.S. soil. "I'm sorry you came all the way up here," Guerrmo began. "I wish we could help. If only she had been

taken on U.S. soil and lured to Mexico, we could do something then." He seemed genuinely disappointed that the agency
could not help. But to me it was just another door shut in my
face.

My parents waited in the foyer in the downstairs lobby.
Being the precious parents they were, they sat waiting for
three hours. As I approached, my eyes began to well up with
tears. "Mom, Dad," I began. "They can't help us. Brittany
wasn't taken on American soil and lured to Mexico; she was
taken in Mexico," I continued as my mom put her loving arms
around me.

"It's OK, Vanda," my dad said. "We're going to find someone who will help you. After all, you are an American.
Brittany is an American. Someone should care enough to
help."

"Well, Dad," I said. "Let's hope so." We walked down the
steps and headed to FBI headquarters.

Now there's a building with daunting security! Several
armed guards were stationed outside. Once inside the building,
we couldn't walk more than 20 feet before a guard asked for
our pass or security clearance. I spoke calmly to the guard and
told him that I wanted to speak to an agent. We waited and
waited. Finally after about an hour, an agent appeared and
escorted me back to a small room.

The agent, Mark, ushered me into an interrogation room
with a two-way mirror. We sat right up next to the reflective
glass. I had an eerie feeling as I sat up next to the two-way
mirror. I knew someone was watching me. *What were they
thinking behind that glass?* I wondered.

After I told him the story, he asked me questions. "How
much do you know about Aldo?"

"Just what he told us, which was probably mostly fabricat-
ed," I said.

"Does Aldo have a passport?" he questioned.

"I have no idea. He told us that he didn't, but he could've been lying," I answered.

"Has he asked for any ransom money?"

"No, but Brittany asks for money frequently. We send it to her because we're trying to track her location," I said.

Mark looked a bit puzzled. "Do you know why she keeps asking for money?" he asked.

"No, I don't. I just assumed they needed it. Aldo knew that we wouldn't refuse," I said.

"What do you expect from the FBI?" The last question took me by surprise. I sat quiet for a moment. Tears began to well up in my eyes. Despite the fact that I knew I was being watched from behind the reflective glass, I looked into Mark's eyes and began, "I thought you would help me find her. We don't know where to turn. No one will help us. I thought you might." I said in a quiet voice as I looked down at my lap and questioned whether we would ever find someone to believe us.

"Well, madam, we don't have the authority to just look for anybody anywhere. We have to have special permission to enter into Mexico on official business."

Oh, boy, I thought. *Give me the bad news.*

"We don't have jurisdiction in Mexico. Our hands are tied," Mark said. "I wish I could help you. My heart goes out to you," he continued. "Maybe a private detective could help you," he said.

"We've tried that twice already. Neither one of them worked out," I said with disappointment.

"I have several contacts in Mexico. Let me see if I can find out anything at all. I'll let you know," he said as he handed me his card.

"OK, I appreciate anything you can do," I said with a heavy heart as I gathered my belongings.

As I approached them, my parents could detect further disappointment. Walking through security, I shook my head *no* and looked down at the floor. They were trying to be strong for me, but their tender presence only drew out my aching spirit. Dad gently touched my arm and said in a loving voice, "No luck here either? We still have an appointment with the State Department this afternoon. They have to listen," he said with confidence.

Famous last words. No one has to do anything, least of all listen.

The security at the State Department was even more unnerving than the personnel at FBI headquarters. No one was allowed past the initial entrance into the building without an appointment or security clearance. Purses, coats, and persons were searched unless one had a security clearance. Even those individuals had to walk through a metal detector.

After checking in at the front desk, I was escorted to a waiting (holding) area. I waited for almost an hour, without my parents, as they were not allowed in the secured area. As I sat on one of the dozen buttery leather sofas, my heart danced a nervous beat. It fluttered in my chest; I could not calm it. Finally a tall, lean woman wearing a crisp, mint-green suit began to approach. Her chilly and uncaring demeanor resonated through the cold, sterile building. The woman, whom I presumed was a low-level secretary for some high-ranking official, made her way over to me and began to speak.

I stood up and thought she would escort me to her office. She remained standing. I sat back down, but she did not sit. She loomed over me and held a copy of the *TV Notas* magazine as she spoke in curt sentences.

"Mrs. Terrell, what can you tell me about this article?" I tried to explain, but she interrupted me, "Well, I understand that your husband and son think your daughter just ran away."

"What?" I asked with confusion. "My husband doesn't think Brittany ran away," I continued.

"Are you sure? Well, I just spoke with Mr. Ramirez at the American Embassy. He got the impression that both your son and your husband think that your daughter ran away. Maybe you and your husband should get your story straight and agree on it before you barge in here and ask for our help. Maybe you should call your husband. It sounds like the two of you need to talk. That will be all," she said with arrogance in her voice.

At that moment she turned and walked away with an air of superiority surrounding her. *Well, thanks a lot, missy!* I said to myself with a smirk and turned-up lip. *Thanks a lot, Miss Government of the United States. The same United States where I pay taxes and vote and support my President . . . . Thanks a heck of a lot*, I screamed in my head as I walked on the gray marble floor. Too bad I lacked the courage to tell her off.

I waited until I got outside before I fell apart. My parents quickly followed me out of the austere building. "Mom," I began between sobs, "she said that her notes from Mr. Ramirez's conversation show that Mike thinks she ran away." Mom shielded me from the guard's probing eyes.

"He doesn't think that. I know he doesn't think that," Mom said with tenderness.

"Or does he?" I asked in a daze. My head reeled with disappointment. I had counted on someone here in Washington to help me, but they treated me as though I was the criminal. My parents, especially my dad, horrified at the treatment I had just received, wanted to tear the woman apart limb from limb.

"Vanda," my dad began. "I want to go in there and speak to that woman." Dad was angry. He was cursing at her, or at the air. Maybe her ears were burning. We sat on a cement planter outside the State Department and wondered how a day that began with such promise could turn into an abyss where hope could never dwell.

We drove back to the hotel in silence. I could never repay my parents for the gentle kindness they showed by standing with me through this horrendous ordeal. On returning to the hotel, I was mentally exhausted and didn't want to think, but another problem had arisen: my stepmother-in-law had just died.

As I spoke to Mike about the day's events, anger welled up in my spirit. *How could he have double-crossed me like that?* I thought. I wanted to confront him, but I had to be an adult as we had another issue at hand: his stepmother's death. Mike and I tried to discuss where we were going to meet in Dallas for the funeral, but anger at the possibility of him turning on me permeated my soul. *I hate him*, I thought but only for an instant. Tears welled up my eyes. No, I didn't really hate him. My loneliness, frustration, and self-pity clouded my mind.

Mom and Dad said their goodbyes. I was off to Dallas. At that moment, I felt as if everyone had turned on me: first my son and now my husband. But I had to keep it bottled up inside until we could sit down and discuss the events that had just transpired. As one knows, the media and the government have a way of drawing their own conclusions. As I boarded the plane, issues of Brittany's disappearance and Mike and Chris's version of the truth only brought more questions to my mind. But we had a funeral to attend. Later I would approach Mike with my questions.

Being with family even at a time such as this comforted me. Staying with Mike's dad was as good for us as it was for him. The funeral was tough, but the feuding between the families was almost more than I could bear. My psyche was fragile enough; now we had to listen to family members bicker about who was going to ride in the family limo and who was getting what in the will. Mike and I didn't want anything except to find Brittany. The rest of the clan could have all the diamonds and nice jewelry they wanted. In the big scope of things, stuff was of little significance. I had cleared my soul of longing for material possessions, but now the funeral and all of the attitudes revealed how inconsequential all those matters really were.

The disparity between how Mike and I felt about Brittany's disappearance did not reconcile itself. The ill feelings brought about accusations directly aimed at each other's most venerable spots—our hearts. Like many others, Mike was beginning to think that perhaps Brittany *did* run away voluntarily. He believed this partly because she did communicate with us but mainly because people who remained objective believed it. No one in the immediate family could agree Brittany was in fact in danger, thusly, dissension ensued. Because he does not give up easily, the devil began to work his diabolical maneuvers—on our strong family ties.

Chapter 17

Columbo in Cowboy Boots

While we were in Plano, we met with Pastor Randy. Even though most of the hype concerning our story had begun to fade, people still inquired as to Brittany's whereabouts. On a biweekly basis FOX News still ran updates.

Pastor Randy spent a good deal of time talking to Chris about our spirits. He remained concerned about the toll the stress was having on our marriage and our well-being. I will be the first to testify that the ongoing stress for the past 100-plus days had turned us into walking zombies. We were numb from hurt, disillusionment, and betrayal. I felt like a dry desert with nothing to give—void of any human emotion. Mike and I didn't know how much longer we could continue in our present state of existence. Both of us lost weight, didn't sleep regularly, and began to doubt our own judgment.

Pastor Randy concluded that we were caving in inside, even though we were desperately trying to put up a front for others. When he looked into our eyes, he no longer saw the bright fire that once burned. Our passion for Christ and for living long ago had been replaced by an instinctual desire of mere survival.

Mike and I were barely alive; Pastor Randy recognized it. Thank God he was able to see through us. As our meeting concluded, the pastor strongly recommended that we move back to Plano.

He began, "Mike, I can see just by looking at you guys that you're dying. You need to be around people who love you. We can surround you with love and support. In Mexico you are isolated. I'm afraid you will continue to deteriorate into a mere shell of who you once were."

At hearing these words I began to weep softly and to tremble. *How can he see that?* I thought. I got up every morning and went through the motions of life—a life with no joy or laughter, no intimacy or love.

These days of torment killed my naïve spirit. But I didn't want others to know I was in such a shape, I tried to be strong and put on a front for others. We listened to our pastor's sweet and caring voice as he expressed his concerns. Reluctantly we agreed. We had to leave Mexico.

"Pastor Randy," Mike said with resignation. "We have to do something. I don't think we can do it by ourselves anymore. I think it's time to go home in spite of our promise to remain in Mexico until we find her. We may never find her," he said with tears welling up in his eyes. We were losing hope.

Just when we were at our lowest point, God showed up again—this time in a BIG WAY. Pastor Randy was such a faithful pastor. His first priority was to us. The next day he asked us to meet again. This time it was about Brittany. Puzzled, we entered his office. He began, "I have some good news for you. I didn't want to say anything yesterday because I want you two home first and foremost, but a security consulting firm has expressed an interest in taking your case."

Mike and I listened, but we were weary and worn. The trust factor was nonexistent. *Would it work?* we wondered. "Will he really help us?" I asked. We had been duped, lied to, and taken advantage of. We weren't getting our hopes up again just for more disappointment, but we listened.

"I spent an hour on the phone talking with Mr. Guidry. He's different," our pastor began. "He contacted us. He's expensive, but he swears he will find her. He has a 98-percent success rate."

Wow, now that's incredible news, I thought. Pastor Randy gave us the information he knew so far. Mike Guidry was an ex-state trooper who lived outside of Houston. His company specialized in extracting children of high-profile parents. He rescued children of movie stars, diplomats, and the like. Well, we weren't what one could call *high-profile parents,* but his service did sound interesting.

Expensive seemed to be an understatement! His usual retainer was $80,000 just to start researching. Then after two weeks, if he needed additional time, another $80,000 was due. But he promised he could find her in two weeks. Except for the money part everything sounded too good to be true. Where in the world were we going to find that kind of money? That's just when God showed up.

Unbeknownst to us, while we visited with Pastor Randy, Mike Guidry was already on his way. A meeting was about to transpire. When Guidry arrived, we were amazed at his appearance—not your stereotypical state trooper: burly and tall. He was only about 5-foot-6. Let me just say I thought he was a little short for the gunslingin' ranger type. Even through his expensive suit, one could see that his physique was well-tuned; a broad chest was evident through his tailored jacket. As he stepped into the office, a beautiful blonde walked in behind him.

Kind of strange to bring your girlfriend to a potential client interview, I thought as she entered. *But hey, if he can find Brittany, he can bring anyone his little ole' heart desires.*

The next hour was a discussion on the disappearance, the emails, the magazine, the fax, the letter, the pictures, and the other investigators—all of it! We hoped this would be the last time we had to go through everything again. Questions were asked and answered. Then Guidry said, "Give me two weeks and $25,000, and I can find her."

"But I thought your initial fee starts much higher," Mike inquired. "Just how do you plan on finding her?" he continued.

"Mr. Terrell," Guidry began. "I have contacts all over the world. Contacts in Mexico are already in place, so I don't have to start from scratch. Besides, this is what I do for a living," he said with confidence. "I extract people from all over the world. I go into terrorist countries. I locate children who have been abducted from their parents, where hundreds of thousands of dollars in ransom are involved. I can find your daughter!" he said with assurance.

Excitement and hope lay under the surface, but Mike and I were scarred from broken promises and didn't want to be swindled again. Guidry looked at us both and said, "You're nice people. You both seem to have wonderful hearts. I hate this happened to you. I want to help." He spoke humbly. "Pastor Randy already told me what a great couple you are. I know you guys don't have any money. The least I can do is to give you a break on my fee," he continued.

Sitting across from Mike and me, Guidry looked us squarely in the eyes and said, "Now I have to ask you. What if she doesn't want to come home?"

That thought had never entered our minds. Dumfounded, Mike said, "Well, just take her anyway."

"OK," Guidry said. "But be aware of what you're asking. I may have to drug her to get her on the plane. Her reluctance could cause us some problems with Mexican customs and security."

My stomach began to flutter as it tied itself in a big knot. The thought of Brittany not wanting to return home never occurred to us and brought a whole new element into the picture. We had always planned on her returning home voluntarily. We had been down this road before. I didn't want to get my hopes up if he was going to walk away without her.

With my heart racing, I asked, "Will you still get her even if she doesn't want to return?" I looked into Mike Guidry's eyes for a glimmer of understanding of the hell we had been through.

Guidry spoke as honestly as he could. "Listen, guys, she's been under this man's influence for five months now. We have no idea what transpired during all this time. We have to be prepared for the worst, that's all," he concluded. "It's going to be a lot tougher to bring her across the border if she's fighting me. One of you may have to fly down once I find her and help me get her returned," he said. "Now, I have another question. What are going to do with her when you get her back?"

We had never let our minds go there before either. We had been stuck in "find-her" mode. We never considered a reluctant daughter or what we would do with her once she arrived here.

Pastor Randy spoke with wisdom, "Mike, we need to have a plan in place after her return. She is not going to be ready to just resume life as it was before without some type of counseling and debriefing." He was right. We had no idea what condition Brittany would be in once she was located.

Finding her indeed would bring about a whole set of new problems. My mind couldn't go there just yet. I first wanted to bask in the idea of Guidry's locating her. After a while all the questions seemed to be asked and a basic plan was put into place. Guidry would call us once he had a chance to look over all the evidence.

Arm in arm, Mike and I walked out of the office. We were hopeful once again. Life seems so strange. Here we were spending all of our retirement money and sacrificing our health and our marriage to find a daughter who perhaps didn't want to be found in the first place. A parent's love remains unwavering in the midst of trials and tribulation. Our resolve remained strong. Our purpose was clear: to see Brittany face to face and wait for possible rejection. That would be the ultimate rejection—for her to look us squarely in the face and say, "I don't want to live with you. I don't love you. Leave me alone . . . ." But my heart wasn't ready to accept this.

While Guidry returned to Houston to begin working on the case, we prepared ourselves to move back to Plano. Once back in Bacalar, leaving this dark region where witch doctors still ward off evil spirits with voodoo dolls seemed like a good decision. Irony, sweet irony, played its hand as we were packing. The few possessions we owned lost their importance. With full hearts and spare belongings we had arrived to help the Latino people. Now we felt as if we didn't even need those few items that remained with us. Now we were leaving with even less—broken hearts. Rosie became the recipient of my Singer sewing machine, a roaster, medical and dental supplies, food, dishes, and the like. Our big red trailer, much like the two of us, was almost empty when we pulled out of Bacalar.

Life has an amusing way of sorting one's priorities. When we arrived in this desolate Mayan community, we were ready to save everyone there. Now, we were the ones who desperately needed saving. Our spirits were crushed, our dreams shattered. But we still had each other; that was a real miracle in itself.

The roads in Mexico are rudimentary at best. Many roadways have potholes so big, a truck could get lost in them. Because of the lack of any type of drainage system, debris lines the dusty trail and leaves little room for automobiles. The arduous, three-day trip was made a little easier as we listened to our praise-and-worship CD's.

Once we arrived back in Plano, we were faced with a daunting question: Where were we going to live? Mike's dad owned a duplex that had become available just days before our arrival. We moved in, if you could call it that. We owned a bed, a kitchen table, and three blue bins full of summer clothes. We had no jobs and little money—a far cry from where we stood the previous year. If we weren't so beat up and broken, our situation might have even been comical, but not now. God always provides a way. I learned a long time ago that you can't outgive God. He never fails to show up.

Our church family dropped by with trunkloads of stuff: lamps, small tables, towels, pots and pans, and dishes. For at least two weeks various items arrived on a daily basis. We had so much stuff, we had to store much of it in an extra bedroom. While I was busy nesting, Guidry was busy getting a line on Brittany's location. Mike emailed Brittany to tell her that we had moved back to Plano and provided our phone number and address.

The contacts that Guidry previously outlined were minuscule compared to the actual services and contacts he possessed. The IP addresses held more information than I ever knew. Guidry contacted the main Internet service provider in Mexico to find out exactly how emails and such were transmitted. Evidently all emails ingoing and outgoing went through a central station in Mexico City. Archaic and tedious, this method of sending emails only made tracking the exact location more difficult.

Since all of the emails we had received were sent through a Yahoo account, Guidry contacted the CEO of Yahoo and asked for his assistance in retrieving the IP location. I was in awe of the fact that in only one phone call he was actually speaking to Yahoo's CEO. Unbeknownst to me, an email can be tracked back to the exact computer from where it was sent. Amazing! Yahoo, based in California, seemed to land on the liberal side when human rights were concerned. Even though

Brittany was only 15, the CEO believed that she had a right to remain anonymous, even if she were in trouble. Guidry hired a lawyer in California to speak to a judge on our behalf. The judge's ruling was issued on the side of the Yahoo conglomerate. Once again another door closed in our faces. But Guidry was persistent. He didn't let a little thing like rulings of privacy deter him from his mission.

One thing Mike Guidry did for us made life a little easier when tracking the emails. He was able to find out Brittany's password. This was HUGE. Even though she didn't write us back very often, I could check her email account to see when she actually opened the emails. With his contacts Mike also was able to work on locating the exact computer from which the emails originated.

This guy was is a REAL INVESTIGATOR! Too bad we had to waste so much time on losers before we happened on the real deal. But then again, isn't that just like God—to show up at one's lowest possible moment?

New York City housed several top-notch hackers who for the small fee of $450 an hour could break any system and find out the needed information. These hackers, if discovered, would have been arrested! Their clandestine work took place after-hours in the darkness. We prayed they wouldn't get caught. Because these emails originated in Mexico, uncovering their true origin became more difficult, but the men were hooked. They had to find the secret. Before long we had accumulated quite a tab just looking for the exact locations of the emails, so the men began to work for free. "We're hooked on finding her. It's like a puzzle just waiting to be solved," said one of the hackers to Guidry.

Finally after many diligent hours, an exact location was uncovered: the university in the Santa Rosa District of Mexico City. Guidry decided to fly down, make some contacts, consider possible plans of escape, check out the Internet Café where the latest email had been sent, and get a general lay of the land. Within two days he was back in Houston. Week one of the promised two-week period was closing, but he had no real leads. We were accustomed to this.

A few days after his return, we received another email from Brittany. Quickly, I called Guidry and forwarded the email to him. It read as follows:

Dear Mom & Dad:

I'm glad you moved back to Plano. You will be close to your friends.

You can move where you want, I am fine. I want you and dad to be happy.

How is Chris? Tell him I miss him. Can you send me some money, please?

I will call you on Thursday nite.

Hugs & kisses,
Brittany

Guidry called me back in moments after he received the email. He began, "Vanda, now this is what I want you to do. Don't take it the way wrong, please. First, I want you to contact the phone company. They can place a tracer on your phone, but they have to have a level-1 clearance from the main office. This might take some time. Maybe we can get it in place before Thursday's phone call. Secondly, when she calls, don't whine or nag at her. Stay calm. Don't try to catch her in a lie. Just let her talk."

Evidently I had a reputation for not being sympathetic while I talked to Brittany. But they were right. Anger at her lies would enrage me, so when I did finally talk with her, I was uptight.

"OK," I said. "I can do that." I hoped I could remain calm and not nag her. Guidry continued, "About the money. Let's hold off for a few days on that so we can hopefully get something in place with Western Union."

"Sounds like a plan," I said. My heart raced as line by line, Mike went through the email. "It looks as if we have a new IPS address on this email. I'll get my men on it right away," Guidry said in closing.

Several hours were spent in utter frustration as I tried to convince the phone company to place a tracer on the phone. Finally I spoke to the right person. A woman on the other end began, "Madam, you need to fax me a request from the police. Call me back on my direct line when you have it. I'll set it up for you." She gave me her number.

I sat at the kitchen table and was flustered once again. *OK, how do I do that?* I wondered. *I wish Mike were here to help me.* "No, you can do this!" I said aloud with resignation. So off to the police station I went.

Once again I replayed the story. After waiting many minutes, I spoke to a cop who was a former missionary. He reminisced about his trip to Colombia, where he spent five months helping the indigenous people build a school in the mountains. Within a few minutes he wrote the letter for me. I was out the door within the hour. Hooray! Now if Brittany would just call.

The month of May was half over. We still were no closer to finding her, or so we thought. It was discovered that the email was routed from another Internet café in Mexico City. I wondered, *Does she spend all of her time moving? Brittany has no way of knowing that we are tracking these addresses. What is she thinking, or is she?* I questioned the sanity of this whole process. Why so many different emails from varied locations? It remained an enigma to us all, but then again most of the past five months had been a trip through the dark wood of Dante's *Inferno*.

Thursday went by. She did not call. Mike's heart was breaking in two. He sat alone on the bed and held the phone in his lap all Thursday afternoon and evening as he waited for it to ring. Behind his blue-green eyes a void existed; a barrier divided our spirits even further than before. Talking had never been his forte, but a fortress around his heart began to surface so as to protect him from future harm. If only that really worked! The silence in the house was deafening despite the white noise in the background from the television neither of us watched.

Even though we had little to do in our new surroundings, Mike sat and simply stared at the blank wall above the television. Frustration at the whole scenario surfaced in both of us. We didn't know where to turn if Mike Guidry didn't work. We may have changed locations, but the devil had a funny way of finding our new address. I think he arrived and opened the door of our new abode for us. I felt as though he said, "Won't you please come in? I've been waiting for you."

A week passed. We were marching time to a nonexistent, beating drum that droned through each day. Brittany had not called. We were approaching the end of week two. She had not sent an email. Because I was isolated and alone, depression began to seep back into my soul. Alone and friendless, jobless, penniless, I sat on the bed day after day and waited for the phone to ring. The silent hell was worse than before. Mike ultimately obtained a job—a purpose of sorts. I had none.

On the following Thursday, in the middle of the soap opera "One Life to Live," Brittany called. Not that I could give a rip about the stupid soap opera, but my guard was down. She hadn't called in seven days. I wasn't expecting her to call then.

She should have known her dad wasn't home; she always preferred speaking to him! So, needless to say, I blew it, again.

The phone rang. It was Brittany. She began, "Hey, Mom! What are you up to today?" He voice was light and happy. Part of me hated her for being so cheerful. I wanted to strangle her neck! The other part of me wept soft tears because I didn't know if she was OK.

With my heart in my throat, I began, "Where are you?" *NO!* I thought. *Don't say that.* I began again, "I'm watching a soap opera. What are you up to today?" *Better*, I thought.

"I'm fine. Mom, is Dad there?" she asked.

"No, Brittany. He's working with Grandpa today," I said as calmly as possible. "We thought you were going to call last Thursday."

"Well, Mom, I was, but I couldn't get away. I tried, but I couldn't, OK?" she said.

"Well, Dad will be home about 5. Do you want to call back then?" I asked.

"I don't think I can," she said. "Are you going to send me some money, or what?" she asked with a touch of anger.

"Brittany, I don't know. How much money do you need?" I asked with tension in my voice. She was making me angry. *The only reason she needs us is for money*, I thought. *All of this heartache and pain, and she calls for money*, I screamed in my head but focused on the task at hand. "How about you email me and let me know," I said.

"OK, tell Dad I love him," she said.

Through tears I whispered, "I love you, Brittany." Waiting for her to return my love, I heard a dial tone. She hung up. She couldn't even return my love with a quiet, "I love you, too, Mom."

I guess I asked too much.

Chapter 18

The Cavalry Storms Huatulco

Eager to see if the tracking device on the phone worked, I called the phone company. Brittany's recent call was from the state of Oaxaca, Mexico. Confused, I called Guidry and filled him in on the conversation. "Mike," I began. "Brittany said that she couldn't get away last Thursday to call us. What do you make of that?" I asked.

Guidry began, "It could mean she is being held against her will, or maybe she just didn't get to a phone."

"The phone call came from the state of Oaxaca," I said. "Do you think they're somewhere in Oaxaca now?" I asked.

"I don't know, but I'll leave this afternoon and head back down there. I'll stay in Mexico City for a day. You talk with Mike and see if he can think of any specific place in Oaxaca they might be. Let's talk tomorrow night," he said.

Guidry flew back to Mexico City that afternoon. He gave us his international phone number in case we heard from her again. One thing we cherished about Guidry: his availability. He seemed to always be just a phone call away. We trusted him implicitly. He had proven himself worthy.

After my phone call, Mike decided to return home. Sitting on our new sofa (our bed) and staring at the TV again, he said with a start, "Vanda, we vacationed in Oaxaca. Remember?"

"No," I said. "When was that?" I questioned.

"When we went on that Club Med/kid's vacation. Remember? The resort was in the state of Oaxaca."

Man, he had a great memory for details! As I thought about it, I did recall that the location of our resort was in

Oaxaca. I began reminiscing about the vacation and thought about our sunny days on the beach. "Do you think they would have gone there?" I questioned.

"Well, it's remote enough. Nothing is there, that's for sure!" Mike said.

He got up off the bed with renewed enthusiasm, "Did Brittany say that she was going to call back tonight?" he asked.

"I don't know, Mike. She really didn't say anything. She did mention the money," I said.

"Why don't we send her $100 and then email her with the tracking number? We'll have to send it to Mexico City, though, because we don't know for sure where she is. That's the last address she gave us," Mike said. His mind was reeling with ideas. "We can't risk sending it to Huatulco. Aldo might figure out that we're getting close!" he said.

I looked at Mike with inquisitive eyes. "We are getting close, aren't we Mike?" I asked. *Wow, I wasn't sure this day would ever be here,* I thought to myself as I reveled in the idea of having her home.

The date was June 3, 2001. Almost four weeks had passed since we hired Mike Guidry. Another $10,000 was due; actually, it was three days past due. Mike had cashed in one of his few remaining retirement CD's. Receiving the check was taking longer than we anticipated. Because he was a true gentleman as well as a professional, Guidry never asked for the money. His job was to find Brittany! But his office staff called on a daily basis.

We had promised Guidry that we would pay what ever he deemed fair, even if we spent the rest of our lives doing so. We weren't so sure that it wouldn't take that long. But we were so close now. We had to find her. We had to uncover the truth, no matter how painful doing so turned out to be. Again, famous last words. Little did we know that the ending would equal the beginning when heartache was concerned.

We received another email from Brittany. It was very informative. We no longer looked at what she wrote but from where the email was sent. It read as follows:

Dear Mom and Dad:

I just wanted to thank you for the money.
It's hard for me to eat without money. I can't work.
There's too much publicity. My picture is everywhere.
I'm thinking about moving to Venezuela soon.
A man told me that I could model down there.
I'll let you know if I decide to go.

Love & Kisses,
Brittany

Mike called Guidry at 8:30 p.m. The phone conversation between Mike and Guidry lasted for more than an hour. I paced around the house and nervously awaited a recap of the conversation. The tracking device on the phone and the recorder were both in working order. The two men discussed the email. Guidry said he wanted to check the new IP address against that of the actual Internet café. He would fly to Huatulco the next day. He had some solid leads that could enable us to find her within the next few days.

Guidry arrived in Huatulco at 4 in the afternoon. After he checked into his hotel, he walked around the square. A gazebo in the center of the square resembled the one in Bacalar. He searched several hours for an Internet café. One was situated about three blocks off the square. Sizing up the customers and the man behind the counter, Mike sat down at a computer near the back of the store. The store was not a café, as these establishments never have refreshments of any kind. I'm not sure why they called it a *café* at all.

Guidry logged onto a computer, checked Brittany's email account, and discussed with the proprietor the performance and usage of current computers. He didn't want to tip anyone off as to his purpose for being in Huatulco, so he made small talk with the owner. He sent an email from his account to my account. For security purposes he had access to all of our accounts. He then checked my account. The email had the same IP address as the email we had just received from Brittany. Guidry knew we were now getting somewhere.

Wanting to keep his identity a secret, he found a tourist-type restaurant for an early dinner. The restaurant happened to be on the square; Guidry watched the comings and goings of the people. He noticed that tourists seemed to be the only ones walking around the plaza. He needed to find another location if he was going to spot Brittany and the others. So, he relocated to a modest taco stand on a street off the square. He stuck out like a sore thumb in his pressed khaki pants and starched, white shirt. He sat reading a newspaper (written in Spanish, which he could not speak) like they do in the movies. As he read, he watched the locals as they passed on the dusty street.

Nothing! He spotted no one and thought he might be in the wrong place. Huatulco covers only about 10 square miles, so for Brittany and Aldo to live here without showing their faces soon would be difficult. But so far, nothing. Even Mike began to get discouraged. Boy, did I know how he felt. The hour was getting late, so he decided to call it a day and start the hunt with a fresh pair of eyes with the morning sun.

Still wound up from the long day, Guidry walked down to the beach to have a beer. As he strolled along the surf, the sound of the waves lapping on the soft sand calmed him. A local band played mariachi music in the distance. He could faintly hear the Latino beat reverberate through the air. Out over the horizon, the stars met the ocean and seemed to be entangled in a dance. Guidry began replaying the emails and the events of the past two weeks. He found questions without answers; that unsettled him. With his breathing calm and his body cooled from the gentle breeze, he walked to his hotel and let sleep take him to a peaceful slumber.

Fatigue from the heat kept Guidry in bed longer than normal. Knowing a bit about Aldo's past and his desire for stardom, Guidry decided to visit several of the hotels along the coastline. Aldo, after all, might be performing in a nightclub. Clubs sprinkled the beach. He spent most of the day in the tourist section of town. He waited until evening to return to the local *barrios* along the square.

At about 8:30 p.m. in Plano. I sat on the bed watching some mindless TV show. Mike was not home when the phone rang: the caller ID said international number. Mike had gone to play golf with several of his buddies. *Good for him*, I thought with a tinge of jealousy. I touched the recorder to turn it on. "Hello," I said.

"Hey, Mommy," Brittany said with unusual delight. "What cha' doing? Mom, guess what? Someone got married today."

"What?" I yelled. *NO!* I screamed to myself. *Stay calm.* My heart began to race. "Oh, really? Wow, that's great. Anyone I know?" *OK, Vanda, now that was a stupid question,* I said as I tried to calm myself.

"Mom, I just wanted to call and thank you for the money," she said. Her voice seemed giddy and light. *Why can't my voice ever do that?* I thought.

"You're welcome, Brittany. So what are your plans? Do you know if you're moving to Venezuela yet?" I asked with as much composure as I could muster.

"No," she said. "Not yet. But I'll let you know if I decide to leave Mexico," she remarked.

LIE . . . LIE . . . LIE, I thought to myself, but I wasn't about to blow it! For once we had the upper hand. "OK, that sounds good. Dad's not here. He's playing golf. He should be home in about 30 minutes," I said.

"OK, well, tell Dad I love him. Talk to you soon," she said and hung up. Holding the receiver close and looking into the phone, I whispered, "I love you, Brittany." Before I hung up the phone, I gently kissed the receiver where moments ago I heard her sweet voice. I wasn't so sure she loved me at all, but right now I didn't care. I could deal with that later.

Think, Vanda, I said as I quickly gathered my thoughts. My heart raced as I listened to the tape carefully and noted the background noises. I heard a band, a lot of people laughing, and church bells ringing. I promptly called Guidry.

"Brittany just called. She thanked us for sending the money. Mike, I heard bells ringing in the background. She said someone got married today. I almost freaked out, but I tried to stay calm," I said rapidly.

"Vanda, I'm standing across the street from a church right now. I hear bells ringing. I'll go over to the little church and see if I spot her," Guidry said. "Let me look around and I'll call you back," he continued.

Wow, this was exciting. *Maybe he'll find her tonight,* I said to myself as I began my pacing routine.

Guidry went to a small corner church off the square. The tiny, mission-style church must have been at least a century old. Cracks ran in varying spider formations up the side of the dusty, brownish building. A weed garden flanked the heavy wooden door that led inside the church.

On entering the sanctuary, a pungent odor attacked his nose. Mike sneezed as the priest approached him. "Hello, can I help you?" the priest said in Spanish.

Guidry, not knowing much Spanish at all, simply held out a picture of Brittany and said, "Have you seen her?"

The priest shook his head *no*. Guidry, angered at the priest's response, said, "Look again. Was she just here?" The priest seemed startled by Guidry's demeanor. Not only did he not speak English, he had not seen the girl in the picture. Guidry stormed out of the church.

As he walked across the street, Guidry glanced up. He spotted another church. He noticed bows and flowers strewn on the ground and wondered, *Is it this church?* He began to cross the cobblestone street and thought, *Maybe there's been a wedding.* He raced across the street. *OK, it's this church,* he said to himself. He bounded the stairs two at a time. The church was empty. It was almost 10 at night. He wondered when the church closed. Guidry called out, "Hello, is anybody here?" A short, chubby man wearing a black robe appeared.

"Have you seen this girl?" Guidry said as he held out Brittany's picture toward him.

"*Sí,*" the priest said.

"Do you speak English?" Guidry asked.

"A little," the priest said.

Mike asked if the girl in the picture got married. The priest said, "*Sí.*"

Guidry then held up a picture of Aldo and asked, "Was this the man she married?"

"No," the priest said. "He much younger," he continued.

"Do you know where I can find them?" Mike asked.

"They went on their honeymoon, but the groom's family lives in town."

The priest gave Mike the address. Away he went. Street signs were nonexistent in this small *pueblito.* Guidry, grasping in the dark, traveled from house to house and thrust Brittany's picture in strangers' faces. The time was after 11 p.m., but Guidry was on a mission. He knew he was close. He wasn't giving up! Not now.

OK, last house, he told himself as he knocked on the door of the home.

A small Mexican boy of about 9-years old answered the door. Guidry thrust the picture in the boy's face. "Have you seen this girl?" he inquired with frustration and anticipation.

"*Sí*," the young lad said. "She's my cousin's new wife.

As Guidry was questioning the boy, a large man loomed in the doorway. "Can I help you?" the man said.

Guidry showed him the picture. The man began to speak in Spanish while the young boy translated. "This girl married my nephew tonight. They are not here. They left on their honeymoon."

Excited, Guidry asked, "Where did they go?"

"To La Hacienda Hotel in Puerto Angel, but they will be back sometime tomorrow. You can return then!" the confused man said.

Guidry could not wait. "*Gracias*," he said and left as quickly as he appeared.

Guidry ran to the rental car and drove to the small town about 45 minutes away. The small, two-lane road was long and wound through the jungle. Darkness surrounded the small, lone blue rental car. On his way he called us and told us the news.

The clock said midnight. The phone rang and startled me. "Hello," I said in a drowsy voice.

"Vanda, I'm sorry to tell you this, but I think I found her. It's not good news. Brittany was married tonight but not to Aldo. She married a young man from Huatulco. I'm on my way now to confront them. I'll call you when I find out something," he said and hung up.

Now Mike and I were really confused. *Where did she meet this man? Why did she get married? Why did she not tell us?* Questions were circling around in my head. We sat in the bed waiting for the phone to ring again. Hours went by. Mike and I drifted off asleep.

Guidry found the hotel. Quickly making his way to the room where the couple stayed, he knocked on the door. The young bride opened the door. She was not Brittany. She was an American. She could have passed for Brittany's twin. Guidry, confused, began to ask the couple questions. He then showed them pictures of Brittany, Alejandra, and Aldo.

The young groom spoke, "I don't remember the girl, but I know the man. He sang and played the piano for our reception." Shocked but elated, Guidry said, "Do you know where he lives?"

"Yes," the groom began. "He lives in apartment 204 on Calle Colotillo in Huatulco. We visited him while we made our wedding plans."

"Thank you so much," Guidry said. "I'm so sorry to disturb you. And congratulations on your marriage!" he said quickly and was off again.

The time approaching 1:30 a.m. Guidry knew he should go back to the hotel, but his adrenaline was pumping. Besides, sleep was not an option—not now when he was so close. He drove back to Huatulco as fast as he could. He located the street and parked his car down the block. In the darkness, as he approached the apartment building, he noticed two large Mexican men who stood outside the gate and were smoking.

With confidence, he approached the men. "*Buenos,*" he said. "I'm looking for Aldo," he said bravely. These two men outweighed Guidry by at least 150 pounds. I would have been petrified, but Guidry remained undaunted. Nothing was going to stop him.

"*Sí*," one of the men said. "Aldo lives here, but you're not getting in to see him if I have anything to say about it."

"I don't think you want to mess with me, fellows," Guidry said as he puffed his chest.

From the corner of his eye Mike noticed a girl walking through the shadows. He glanced at her as she walked down the long, dark street alone. A small street lamp illuminated her figure. As she approached, Guidry recognized her. It was Alejandra! He waited until she moved closer to be sure. Then he called out her name, "Alejandra."

Alejandra looked startled as she eyed the American man. "Do I know you?" she questioned.

"No, but I know you. Brittany's parents sent me," he said.

With that, Alejandra dropped her head and said, "Oh. I knew they would send someone. It was only a matter of time." The two Mexican men moved to stand next to Alejandra—possibly to protect her, if needed.

Staring at Alejandra's eyes, Guidry sneered at her, "Where's Aldo and Brittany?" he asked.

"Inside, sleeping," she said in a nervous voice. "What are you going to do to me?" she asked.

"I don't want you. Just Brittany. Show me where they are NOW!" he exclaimed.

The blue, three-story building was horrific. Debris, discarded clothing, and household items were strewn all over the yard of the complex. Windows were boarded up with scrap pieces of wood. Guidry wondered how anyone could live here, but he remained silent. They approached apartment 204.

Leering at Alejandra he commanded, "Stand here and don't say a word." Petrified, Alejandra didn't make a sound. Her heart raced as she likely wondered whether Guidry would hurt her or whether she would be thrown in jail for her part in Brittany's disappearance.

"Aldo," he yelled. "Are you in there? Come out here. NOW!" No one appeared. He yelled louder, "Aldo, get out here. Don't make me come in there and get your sorry ass!"

Suddenly the door opened. A small man appeared. Aldo's physique was scrawny, as he only weighed about 140 pounds. It was Aldo. He was standing in the doorway wearing only his underwear. A look of bewilderment was on his face, but in his heart, he no doubt knew why he was being summoned. He had waited many months for this day to arrive. He feared I was a woman of my word. I had made a promise to Aldo that I would search for my daughter forever . . . however long that might take.

"Come here!" Guidry commanded. Aldo approached. For once he was speechless. He stood next to Alejandra with his arms crossed. He dared not speak. "Don't move! Stay here!" Guidry commanded.

Mike approached the front door. He walked in and saw Brittany lying on the floor. She was wearing her underwear. Her knees were drawn up into her chest. "Brittany," he called out. "I'm Mike Guidry. Your parents sent me to find you and take you back."

Brittany began to weep. "I knew you would find me. I had a feeling they wouldn't give up until they found me," she said.

"Put your clothes on. I'll wait outside. Are you OK?" he asked.

"Yes," she whispered.

"Well, get dressed. We need to call your parents," Guidry ordered.

As Mike walked out of the apartment, a roach scurried across his shoe. The small room had no furniture, only several mats on the floor that served as beds. Clothes and trash littered the floor. *How could anyone live here?* he thought as he waited for Brittany.

The day was June 6, 2001. The phone rang at 3:33 a.m. "Hello," Guidry said. "I have someone here that wants to talk to you. I found her, but there's something I need to tell you before you talk to her."

My heart pounded. Tears filled my eyes. "She's pregnant," I said. A sickening feeling filled my spirit.

"OK, now you know," He said. "But be kind, please! We don't know what she's been through yet."

He put Brittany on the phone. "Brittany, is it really you?" I said as I began to cry. "Oh, my God, he found you." My heart pounded. "Oh, Brittany, are you okay?"

"Yes, Mamma, you found me. I told you all along that I was fine," she said coldly.

I handed Mike the phone and began to weep into my pillow. Part of me was overjoyed. I could hardly believe that we had finally located her. Part of me was angry. She sounded so cold and aloof. I detected no love in her voice as we spoke. My heart was breaking all over again. I had waited many months for this day. It was finally here; it wasn't turning out at all as I had planned.

Mike spoke to Brittany for a few minutes. Tears fell down his cheeks as he listened to her sweet voice. "I miss you," he said tenderly. "I want to pull you through the phone and hold you, sweet girl."

Mike handed me the phone again. "It's Guidry," he said. "He wants to talk to you."

"Hello," I said through tears.

"Vanda, it's late. Let's all get some rest. Brittany promised me she'd meet me in the morning for breakfast. We'll call you back then," he said. "We'll call you tomorrow at 10. Even though I don't trust him. Aldo promised he would meet me in the morning at a restaurant down the street. I threatened to hurt him if he tried to run. Let's call it a night," Guidry said wearily.

He hung up the phone. I looked at Mike. Gathering me in his arms, we wept. "He's going to call in the morning at 10 a.m.," I said. We had nothing to say. I felt empty. I thought finding her would bring a sense of relief, but I felt rejected and empty.

Mike and I held each other close for a long while before we drifted off to sleep. The mere feat of finding her had driven us for months on end. If we had let go of the search, I think we would have fallen apart. In a way the search itself drove us to wake up every morning and live another day. Mike and I had learned to survive.

Chapter 19

Leaving Empty-Handed

Ten a.m. couldn't have arrived soon enough for Mike and me. Anxiously waiting the appointed hour, I paced around through the den and into the hallway and back. I was filled with nervous energy. Mike sat on our bed and stared through the television. My body, filled with angst, could not remain calm. I believed that the final shoe had not fallen.

"Will Guidry bring her home today or tomorrow?" I asked Mike.

"I don't know," Mike said. "Let's just wait and see what he has to say when he calls."

Ten a.m. arrived and went, but the phone did not ring. The hour approached 11 a.m. Finally, the awaited call. Guidry spoke first. The words he spoke pierced my soul. "Vanda, she doesn't want to come home," he began.

"What? What do you mean she doesn't want to come home?" I screamed.

"She says she loves him and wants to stay with him," Mike said. "We have been talking for a while already. And she's pretty adamant about it. She says that she'll run away if I bring her back."

My heart was breaking! I couldn't believe what I was hearing. "I HATE HIM!!!" I yelled.

"Vanda, calm down. I'll take her, if that's what you guys want. I promised you I would, but under the circumstances, I wouldn't advise it. We'll work something out," Guidry said as I handed the phone to Mike.

I jumped out of the bed and began pacing again. Anger welled up in my throat. Ranting, I began yelling things out loud as I paced around the house. "I hate her! What does she think she's doing? Of course she's coming home. I'm not leaving her down there with that devil man!" I'm not proud of the things I said, but we had just spent the last six months of our lives searching for her, and now this! I couldn't take this disappointment. I didn't know how to wrap my mind around what I was hearing. It made no sense to me.

Mike spoke to Guidry calmly. Then Mike handed me the phone and said, "He wants to talk to you."

Guidry began, "Vanda, you were right about Aldo. While he was telling me how much he cared about Brittany, he was checking out another girl at the restaurant. He told me how he wanted to caress her hair. It made me sick. Here he is with the prettiest girl in town who is about to have his baby, and he's already looking at another woman. He's just about the slickest man I've ever met. I feel like I need to go take a shower, but that doesn't change things. She's not coming home."

Devastated and broken, I asked, "What do you think we should do? Should we leave her down there? I can't stand the idea of not bringing her home. I don't want Brittany around him another minute!" I wanted my precious daughter home.

"I know, but I believe Brittany will run away if I bring her back. Aldo has promised me that he won't lay a hand on her, that he will provide for her, and that he will love the baby," Guidry said.

My heart was breaking all over again. Every word pierced my heart like a cold sword. The idea of Aldo touching her made me nauseous. "I think the best thing for right now is to leave her here. I'm not saying forever—just for now. Vanda, she's young. You should see where they live. I don't think she's going to last down here very long."

176

"Put Brittany on the phone, please," I begged. I didn't know what I was going to say to her, but I had to try and talk some sense into her.

"Mom, I love him," she began. As I listened to her words, my stomach wrenched with anger, but my mouth remained silent as she spoke. She continued, "I know you don't like Aldo and you don't approve of my decision to stay here, but I love him. I don't care how old he is! And I DON'T WANT TO LIVE WITH YOU ANY MORE!"

The words I feared would kill me rang out and seared through my core. My heart raced. As she spoke, I clinched my teeth. For months the search itself enabled us to survive. Now the dream of finding her had turned into another nightmare— perhaps more frightening than the one we were living.

My spirit was crushed. How were we to go on without her? I gathered my thoughts and with a mother's heart pled with her to think about her choice.

"Brittany, are you sure this is what you want? Not Aldo, but you? You're 16. Honey, we missed celebrating your 16th birthday. You've been missing so many months now. How do you know that Aldo is the man you want to spend the rest of your life with?" I asked with as little anger as I could possibly muster under the circumstances.

"Yes, Mom. I want to stay. Don't make me go home. My home is here with Aldo," she said.

Guidry was on the phone again. "Brittany, Aldo, and I have a lot of talking to do. I'm not going to leave her here unless I am 100-percent sure that she wants to stay and that she'll be safe. I'll call you this evening and we can talk some more.

"OK, whatever." I said. My body, mind, and spirit shut down. Disappointment and hurt filled my soul. Guidry hung up. I handed the phone to Mike. I lay on the bed and felt broken, angered, and wounded. "Now what?" I asked.

Mike looked at me with hollow eyes and said, "I'm going to get a shower and go to work."

"Yeah, OK," I said as jealousy passed through my soul. He had somewhere to go to escape this hell pit, even if for only a while. I, on the other hand, had nowhere.

Mike went to work. I needed to make some phone calls. I called my mom and told her the news. My mom could be extremely wise at times. She sensed that I didn't need anyone telling me "I told you so" right now. She just listened. She comforted me. I was glad I called.

Next, I called Chris, the son who gave up two months of his life and missed his college graduation to look for his sister. *How is he going to take the news?* I wondered. All I can say is, better than I!

"Mom, it's OK. Let her stay down there for a while. I know Brittany. She's not going to want to live in those squalid conditions for very long. It'll get old soon enough. She'll come home," he said lovingly. He, too, could sense my pain.

Next, I called our pastor to let him know that we found Brittany. Pastor Randy was hurt. He felt as though he and the congregation had been duped. Well, we all had. He was not happy about our decision to leave her down there. I tried to explain to him that we believed it was the best thing to do under the circumstances. After I filled him in on the whole scenario, he, too, believed it was the only choice at the present. He thanked me for telling him the truth.

What's wrong with me? I wondered. *I'm the only one crushed here. I can't stand it!* The search had ended; the search that had driven us for months was finally over. But my heart remained broken. With no purpose or sense of belonging, I sat at the computer and played Solitaire. My mindless game: Solitaire. I could click the buttons for hours and never think about anything except . . . *red three on the black four.*

Hours ticked by. The phone rang sometime in mid-afternoon. It was a reporter from FOX News. She had spoken to the church and been given an update of sorts. She asked me to please let her know when we found Brittany. The station had put a lot of time and money into the story. It was still receiving dozens of inquires a day from its audience. The station wanted to do an interview when we found Brittany.

What do I do? I wondered. We still didn't know how things were going to play out, but I promised the reporter that I would call her. I consented to an interview when the time was right. I waited for Mike's return. Evening arrived; Mike returned home.

After dinner, Guidry called. He recounted his day with Brittany, Aldo, and Alejandra. Guidry spoke to Aldo at length about his expectations. He promised Aldo that if he ever mistreated Brittany in any way, he would fly down and Aldo's body would never be found. Guidry was stuck between a rock and a hard place. While his heart went out to us, he knew in his gut that he had no easy answer to this scenario.

Calmer and more composed now, I asked if I could please speak to Brittany. I needed answers to so many unanswered questions. Apologies needed to be made. Both Aldo and Brittany had some explaining to do. But the two of them believed they had no need. No questions were answered, no apologies were made, and no explanations were given. Like it or not, we had to accept things at face value.

"Hello, Brittany. I have to know something. Why did you tell Ernestina that we were very bad people? What have we ever done to you to make you say that?" I questioned.

"Oh, Mom, that was Aldo. He made me write that," she said with no sadness or hint of remorse in her voice.

With my stomach in a knot, I asked another difficult question. "Why did you let us believe you were a prostitute or a dancer or watched by the police? What was the purpose of all those clandestine emails you sent? We were worried sick about you. How long were you going to keep up this charade?" I asked, but I wasn't sure I wanted to know the answer.

She answered this question with a sharp response.

"Forever, or until you found me, whichever came first," she said with no remorse. "I didn't want you to find me. I'm happy," she said as if her happiness made everything all right.

"Oh, my gosh!" I thought. I couldn't believe what I was hearing. This was worse than not knowing: to be rejected by your own daughter! I'd had enough, so I handed the phone back to Mike. "Here, you talk to her," I said.

Brittany promised her dad that she would call every Wednesday night between 8 and 9 p.m. She also promised she would notify us if they decided to move somewhere else. And most importantly she swore that she would call if and when she ever wanted to return home. We ended it there.

We would forever remain grateful to Mike Guidry for finding Brittany. We felt some comfort in knowing she was safe, or so we thought! Guidry returned home the next day. He called as his plane landed. I told him about FOX News and asked his advice. "This didn't turn out like we planned, but I think we should meet with the reporter and tell her the truth. What do you think?" I asked.

"Well, Vanda," he began, "my experience with the press has been that if you're not truthful with them, and they don't like what you tell them, then they will search for their own ending," he said. "I think you should meet with them and tell them what happened," he said.

"I'm so tired of being lied to; I'm done with lies. We have nothing to hide. I think so, too," I replied. "Oh, by the way, the reporter asked if you would be willing to be a part of the interview. I told her I didn't know and would have to ask you.

What do you think?" I remembered Guidry sharing with us that part of his success is his anonymity, so I wasn't sure he would want to appear on television.

"Part of my success is the fact that I am anonymous. I don't do interviews," he said. "I don't need my face on TV. I don't need people knowing who I am. It's part of why I am able to do what I do. People don't know what I look like. I'd like to keep it that way."

"OK, that's fine with me. I'll call and let her know," I said as I hung up.

I called the reporter. We set up to do the live interview in our sparse den with hardly any furniture at all. I called and told Mike about the interview. He said he would be home early. We would be on the 5 o'clock news! Unbeknownst to us, the station began running trailers advertising that Brittany had been found and that the story would run that afternoon.

At 4 p.m. the reporter's car pulled up to the house. As I opened the door to help the crew, I saw Mike Guidry's car pull up. Confused, I asked, "What are you doing here?"

Cutting his eyes toward the beautiful, blonde reporter, he said, "She can be pretty convincing. But I'm not sure if I'm going to appear on camera," he continued.

"OK, come on in," I said. The phone rang. I ran inside to answer it. "Hello," I said.

"Vanda, it's Pastor Randy," he said in a curt voice. "I understand you are doing an interview today with FOX 4 News. What are you going to tell them?" he asked. "I'm in Colorado for a convention. I can't get there today. Why don't you wait until I return before you do the interview?"

"We're going to tell them the truth, Pastor," I said very plainly.

"Are you sure you should tell them that she's pregnant?" he asked.

"The story doesn't make any sense if we don't tell them that. Why would we leave her down there if she weren't pregnant with Aldo's baby? I'm not going to lie to them, Pastor Randy. We are so tired of being lied to. It's time to just tell the truth!" I said with conviction.

"Well, I'm just wondering if it's wise to tell them about a baby. Vanda, maybe we should wait on that part of the story," he said.

"I'm sorry, Pastor Randy. Mike and I have talked about this. We have nothing to hide. We've been tricked; we all have, but we're weary. We want it all out in the open," I said.

"OK," Pastor said, "I trust your judgment. Whatever you think is best. We love you guys." Then he hung up the phone.

I understood his frustration. We all wanted a different ending—one in which we were able to rescue her from trouble's grip. The ending was not our choosing. We simply had to play the cards we were dealt. I empathized with our pastor's hurt and desired a different conclusion to our saga, but as far as I was concerned, we didn't have one.

As the reporter set up, I relayed my phone conversation to Mike and Guidry. Nervous about how the reporter and the TV audience would deal with the truth, my stomach churned. I didn't want us appearing to be bad people. I didn't want others to think they had been duped, too. Many of these people had given money. Even more of them had prayed for Brittany's safe return. The ending, I was afraid, might anger some of the viewers.

The session lasted about 45 minutes. Guidry appeared on camera. I shared a calendar with the audience. Every morning for the past 150 days I would rise and place a large "X" in the space usually reserved for daily activities. As I looked at the calendar, sadness almost overcame me. Flipping through the months, no special days such as Brittany's 16th birthday or

Mother's Day and the like were observed. Only "X's" dotted the calendar. Although doing so was difficult, I tried to remain strong while I was on camera.

As the interview closed, I looked squarely into the camera. I apologized for the ordeal and thanked the thousands of people who cared about our plight and us. "Please, I want to say thank you to everyone that loved us and prayed for us and helped us financially. Mike and I are devastated it ended this way. We love our daughter and wish she would come home. Each of you will always have a special place in our hearts. Thank you for caring for us. Thank you . . . ." Then tears fell and a lump appeared in my throat. This made continuing to speak nearly impossible. The taping ended.

Mike and I were humbled that so many strangers had reached out to us with their prayers and their donations. Before she left, the reporter asked if I would keep her updated on Brittany. She wanted to be informed if Brittany ever returned to the United States. That day would be a long time off.

Now the time arrived for Mike and me to pick up the pieces, such as they were, and to try and move on with our lives. Anger, rejection, and disappointment are not easily put aside. A very long time would pass before our spirits would begin to heal from this ordeal.

Mike and I had a wounded marriage. But at least we were alive. Brittany was alive. We had found her, but neither of us was ready to see her just yet. That, too, would take a long time to occur. The road that Brittany chose in Mexico was rocky and full of heartache for her and for us.

Little did we know that another nightmare loomed just around the corner—several more years of Brittany's living with Aldo.

Chapter 20

Butterfly Kisses from Above

More than five years have passed since our horrific nightmare began. Allowing Brittany to stay in Mexico turned out to bring new troubles. Some new catastrophe with her well-being seemed to surface every couple of months. Months of therapy and Christian counseling were necessary before Mike and I could stop blaming ourselves for what had transpired. The road was rocky. At times, I thought I would never return to a world in which happiness reigned once again. Thoughts of suicide resumed. While my friends and family were reaching out to me, I was pushing them further and further away. I did not want anyone to know of my fragile state. Once again I pretended to be strong. I had trouble dealing with the fact that our saga did not have a storybook ending.

I tried to pick up the pieces, but I felt like an old Raggedy Ann doll—limp and lifeless. Hollow inside, I wore a painted-on smile for the world to see. While the world saw a smiling woman trying to move on, I longed to scream, "I'm dying in here. Will you help me?" But I remained silent. Silent isolation moves like a mist. While it is visible, it lacks any substance. The mist of my isolation permeated my being, but I remained silent and spoke to no one about my diseased soul—a soul that needed tenderness and love.

Reactions from others about our decision to leave Brittany in Mexico arrived with criticism. Bewildered, people questioned why we let her remain there. They tried to be kind. But their cursory attempt at kindness drove me mad. Likewise, people were shocked that Aldo was still alive. We received many offers from people who wanted to go and "make Aldo disappear." As people listened, Mike and I believed this was not an option. Mike and I would attempt to explain our reasons, but unless you've lived it, understanding our situation was impossible. Church friends didn't know what to say when they saw us. They often chose the trite words that pierced my heart: "At least you know where she is!"

What kind of comfort is that? I would scream in my head. I needed great fortitude not to say back to these well-wishers, "Let me take your child and place her under someone else's influence in a foreign country in a rat-infested hovel and then say to you with a smile, 'At least you know where she is'!" I found no comfort in their empty words. Many months of self-talk and working through my anger would pass before I could genuinely look on that comment, simply smile, and say "Thank you."

Through these intervening years we have learned many things about Aldo. Brittany was not the first teen-ager he led astray—she may have been the fourth. We learned that Aldo had not spoken to Alejandra for 23 years before his calls pleading with her to move to Bacalar to get close to Brittany. Alejandra had been an infant when Aldo had last seen his daughter. He was able to persuade Brittany to leave with him with an initial promise of making her a model. He promised a quick, two-week Mexico City trip in which she would become famous.

Once he isolated Brittany from our parental loving guidance, he filled her head with fantastic ideas. He told her that we never wanted her to be a normal teen-ager but that we wanted to smother her. These ideas reeled in Brittany's head and were juxtaposed by our gentle supervision and loving hand trying to steer her through her teen years successfully.

Brittany was flattered by the attention Aldo lavished on her. Growing up, Brittany suffered from low self-esteem despite our best efforts to build her up. As a child she had worn glasses and always commented on how "ugly" she looked. Aldo fed Brittany's desire for validation and thrilled her ego with compliments.

Aldo assured Brittany that Mike and I were holding her back from all her dreams and desires. He assured her that we wanted her to remain sheltered, go to college, and not let her live her own life. Aldo twisted into a distorted tale every conversation we had while he was in Bacalar.

For many months Brittany relied on Aldo for everything: food, shelter, love, and acceptance. She bought his distorted tale and never let us in on what she was going through. Brittany and Aldo lived in a world of deception.

In spite of the agreement Brittany and Aldo struck while Mike Guidry was in Huatulco, we rarely spoke with her. But she did call regularly for money. Even the basic needs such as food, water, rent, and a phone were luxuries for them. Aldo's attempts to succeed as a musician were lame at best. Aldo performed at nightclubs and *barrios* in the region. Times were lean for them and disappointing for us. We remained in Texas; she remained in Mexico. We always sent money when she asked. We wanted to do more than send money, but we needed time to heal. Daily we had to live with the reality that we left her down there. Living with the fact that we chose to leave her in Mexico, far from our tender arms, was not easy.

In December 2001 Brittany called and asked me to fly down and stand by her side while she gave birth to Aldo's baby. She would have been a junior in high school, but instead, at 16 she was about to give birth. She was a child herself. As she spoke, images of my standing next to Aldo while

186

my first grandchild was born flooded my mind. *How could I stand next to Aldo?* I wondered. *How can I smile and pretend I am happy about the whole situation?*

Despite the fact that I longed to see Brittany, I couldn't do it. Not yet. The wounds of betrayal were too fresh. Mike and I did not go to Mexico. Neither one of us was ready to be in the same room with Aldo. Many sessions of therapy would be necessary before we could begin to entertain the idea of visiting her there. Too many hurtful words had been exchanged. While Mike and I longed to see our daughter, we knew all that had transpired crushed our hearts. Time was needed for us to heal.

During the next couple of years we reached out to Brittany with money and gifts for birthdays and Christmas for her and her two daughters, Marie Lou and April. The door was always open for her and the girls when she wanted to return home.

The decision to leave her in Mexico plagued us. As Mike and I were working on healing our marriage and our hearts, Brittany's pleas for money always made us feel guilty and caused a tinge of anger to surface within us. This made the healing process difficult at times. Sometimes we believed as soon as we took a step forward toward healing, we would react to Brittany's predicaments and take two steps back.

I'm not sure how many miracles each of us is allotted in this lifetime, but I have experienced more than my share. I could have never done this alone; in fact, I take no credit for who I am today. The Scriptures say, *All things are new in Christ Jesus*—including me. Over the years I laid my pain and anger at His feet, only in my humanness to pick it up again. For many months I struggled with the pain and the search for forgiveness.

In July 2003 we made a crucial decision; the time had arrived to see Brittany. She was 17-years old and had two children. We flew to Huatulco. Our son, Chris, and Mike's dad,

Floyd, went with us. Mike and I were nervous about the encounter. We were beginning to realize that Brittany might not ever return to Texas. Besides, we now had two grand-daughters; we longed to meet them.

We walked up to the blue gate which led to Brittany's apartment. My stomach swirled. *Buenos!* Mike said as we approached the gate. Brittany leaned out of the front window and beamed at our presence. We entered the small apartment. Furnishings were sparse, but the apartment was clean. The babies were precious.

After we exchanged hugs and kisses, Brittany showed me around her home. The refrigerator had no food, only beer. The pantry was bare save one stale box of cereal; nothing was there to feed those precious babies. Brittany and Aldo did not have a stove on which to boil water or to prepare dinner. The kitchen sink was inoperable. Brittany and Aldo slept on a deflated air mattress with a hole in it. The two girls slept in hammocks.

We stayed three days. We laughed loudly and hugged often. The days flew by. We so enjoyed getting to know our granddaughters. Mike and I did what we could to make their lives a little easier. We bought a stove for the kitchen; Mike replaced the sink. We took Brittany to the grocery store. Despite our fears, Brittany appeared happy. We weren't sure how she survived these conditions, but she always was a stub-born little lady.

As we said our goodbyes, Mike asked Brittany if she want-ed to return home. "My life is here with Aldo," she said. With that, we left.

Mike and I felt good about our visit. We had made the first move toward reconciliation—one that would be met with more heartache. Brittany and Aldo continued to struggle financially. To be sure, the road was tumultuous.

In May 2004 we decided to make a family portrait. Chris flew down from Jackson, WY. Picture day was fast approaching. *But what would a family portrait be without Brittany? I wondered.* I didn't have to wonder long. One night as the three of us were getting ready to go out to dinner, the phone rang. "Hello," I said.

"Mom, it's me."

"Brittany?" I asked.

"Yeah, it's me. I'm here at the airport. Are you going to pick me up, or what?" she asked. Brittany was at DFW Airport. Aldo had allowed her to join us for our family picture, or so we thought! He kept the girls with him which insured her return. He also had contacted an acquaintance in a nearby suburb to keep an eye on Brittany during her visit.

"How long are you staying?" Mike inquired.

"I don't know; a few days," Brittany said. Wow, we were all together again! What an answer to prayer. Mike and I were in heaven.

Friday was picture day; it was joyous. Brittany was beautiful. Aldo had dyed Brittany's chestnut hair blonde, but the blonde part had begun to fade. The sitting at the studio would long be remembered.

On Saturday afternoon I asked Brittany if she wanted to go for a walk with me. On our walk I could sense Brittany wanted to talk about something. My "mother-radar" was on. I began, "So, did you really fly down here for the family portrait? Or is there another reason for your visit?"

"Mom, I want you and dad to buy me and Aldo a car," she said. "I'm 17. You owe me a car."

My heart pounded, but my mouth remained silent. She continued, "You bought Chris a car when he turned 16. We need a car, Mom."

I searched my mind for the right words. "Well, Brittany, why can't Aldo buy you a car? Besides, how would you get it home?" I asked.

She and Aldo had already planned out the whole scenario. She began, "I'll stay and take driver's ed. And then Dad and I can drive the car to the border. Aldo and the girls will meet us at the border. Then Aldo and I will drive the car to Huatulco."

I couldn't believe what I was hearing. Just when I thought we were healing our hurting hearts, she did this! But I had learned a lot since the whole ordeal began and remained calm.

"Let's see what Dad thinks about this first," I said. Well, Mike did not take the news well. He felt betrayed. Brittany had not matured. She still desired to be "Daddy's little girl" despite the fact that she was living the life of a woman and a mother. We did not buy Brittany a car.

After realizing she wasn't getting her way, Brittany left mad and hurt. She couldn't understand why we would not grant her request. Once again Mike and I were hurt and bewildered. We both wondered how long this hell was going to last.

Attempts were made to heal our wounds over Brittany. But Mike and I seemed to put more effort into the healing than Brittany did. As I said before, the road was rocky and full of holes and heartache. Despite our sorrow we continued to love Brittany. We emailed often, called on a regular basis, and always were ready to help her in any way possible. But we believed that at some point, Brittany needed to reach out to us. All of our attempts to show her our undying love seemed to fall on a hardened heart. Time had arrived to give her some room to grow. Brittany needed to realize that she chose her path. But Mike and I were never too far away. A parent's arms are always there—ready to catch a child when he or she falls.

In March 2005 Brittany decided she wanted to live closer to Texas. She, Aldo, and the two young girls traveled by bus from Huatulco to Juarez to stay with some missionary friends. Traveling through the dusty and litter-filled, rudimentary roads took almost three days. The bus stopped many times for gas, food, and restroom breaks. When they finally arrived in Juarez, Jonathan, the owner of an orphanage and school, went to the bus station and picked them up. Jonathan's family was reluctant to take Aldo in but decided it was the right thing to do. Jonathan and his father hoped that they could minister to Brittany and perhaps eventually convince her to return home. They had grand plans of showing Aldo the error of his ways, but that was not easy.

In July 2005 for my birthday, we went to Juarez to visit Brittany. For several weeks Mike had asked me what I wanted to do for my birthday. I really had no ideas. Mike hinted several times that we could go and see Brittany. Not exactly what I wanted to do for my birthday, but Mike wanted to go so badly. I didn't have the heart to say no. The visit went relatively well.

Brittany, Aldo, and the girls lived in a two-room stucco shack. At least 20 years ago the house had been painted a bright orange. Parts of the gray stucco showed where the paint had been weathered away by the scorching sun and torrential rains. A curtain served as the front door.

While it was 104-degrees outside, the thermometer could have registered 90 degrees inside the small home. The house was adequate for Mexico, and the price was right. It only cost 1,000 *pesos* a month, or roughly $100. The house did have a few quirks, though. The water trickled from a broken faucet in the kitchen, but a hole was in the sink; the water ran onto the cement floor. It had no hot water, no dishes, no food, and no toilet paper. Aldo, however, seemed to have plenty of beer.

As we entered the house, Aldo inquired, "One beer? Vanda, Mike, one beer, yes?"

"No, thank you," Mike managed without exploding.

One beer? I screamed in my head. *NO! I don't want one beer. I want my daughter.* But I remained calm. "No, Aldo, but thanks!"

Mike and I did what we could to make life a little more bearable for Brittany and the girls. We filled the gas tank so they could take hot showers. Mike repaired the washing machine that sat on the front porch. He repaired the sink and patched the hole so water didn't run onto the floor. We bought them groceries and dishes and bought the girls clothes and shoes. It was the least we could do. We gave Jonathan money in case of an emergency.

During the visit, Aldo requested a meeting with us. Jonathan served as the translator and mediator. Aldo wanted to clear the air so we could all be one happy family. *Funny!* I thought. *Not in a million years.*

Aldo must have thought for quite a while about what he was going to say to us. Needless to say the meeting did not go well. As far as I was concerned Aldo could never say anything that would justify his taking Brittany from us.

When I asked him why he took Brittany, he said, "Because I wanted her."

My heart pounded. *What kind of reason is that?* I questioned. Aldo's attempts to justify his actions only infuriated Mike and me.

After many hurtful words and a lot of tears, Jonathan said he would look after Brittany and make sure she was safe. That was about all we could ask for at the moment. On Sunday before we left, Mike pulled Brittany aside and said, "OK, do you and the girls want to come home?" Tears filled Mike's eyes as he looked in his daughter's face.

A long silence ensued. She seemed close to saying, "Yes," but after a long pause, she said, "No, Dad, this is my home."

With broken hearts once again, we drove 10 hours back to Plano and wondered what exactly would be necessary for her to return. We were beginning to doubt if it would ever happen. But all in all, we were both glad we had gone. The girls were precious. I had to give Aldo that; he was the father of two beautiful girls.

Bitterness and anger control us if we let them. If I had remained angry and resentful, who would have suffered? Me, that's who; I would have missed out on my own life. After tragedy and betrayal, we are filled with a spirit of unforgiveness and bitterness. We carry this spirit much like a poison we then spew onto others. This venom dwells in our hearts and separates us from the Father. Only through much counseling, prayer, and supplication could I begin to make headway. On my own I could not forgive Aldo or Brittany. I had to rely on God to first remove the poison from my soul and then to replace it with joy and thanksgiving. Eventually bitterness left me and did not return. Finally, I vowed to let go of the anger, to not pick it up, to not ask why, and to not hold grudges to those who caused me pain: mainly my daughter and Aldo. I had to find a way to be all that God wanted me to be. To do that, I must be whole and healthy and lay my hurt at His feet.

Much to our surprise, Brittany called the next week and said she wanted to return for a visit. We were elated. Maybe we could talk some sense into her and get her and the girls back to Plano where they belonged. She arrived on July 9.

On Sunday we went to church. I felt a great sense of pride as Brittany sat next to me. After church we went home. I began making lunch when Brittany walked into the kitchen and stood next to me. I could sense she wanted to tell me something, so I stopped making the sandwich. I turned and looked at her.

Gazing at the floor with her arms folded tightly across her chest, she began, "Mom, I want to come home."

I was shocked. Silence. Not knowing how to react, I cautiously said, "Really? Well, that's great, baby." My heart was breaking as tears welled up in my eyes. I had waited for more than five years to hear those sweet words.

"No, Mom. You don't understand. I want to start over, without the girls."

Huh? I thought. What did she mean without the girls? I waited for her to continue.

"No one will want me if I have two kids," she said. "I don't want the girls. I want to begin a new life without them." She stopped and hung her head low. Tears pooled in her large, hazel eyes—hurting and weary eyes. With hesitation, she began again, "Aldo can have them, or you can throw them off a cliff. I don't care."

Dumfounded, my heart began to pound as I stood on the cold kitchen floor and wondered whether this was my daughter. "Who are you?" I wanted to ask with judgmental anger, but I remained composed. My head spun with possible reactions. Miraculously, I remained calm.

"Brittany," I began with tenderness in my voice. "Sweetheart, these two precious girls did not ask to be born. You owe them a life. You owe them a chance to be happy. You owe them a future." I took her hands in mine and looked into her hurting eyes. "Let's go get them. You don't want Aldo to have them. They will have no chance for a happy, healthy life with him. Your dad and I will rear them. You, my darling, can live your life. I know that someday you'll want to be their mother. Someday, you'll be ready to care for them. You've been through so much. In many ways you're just a child yourself. You lack the skills or education necessary to rear these girls adequately."

I pulled her into me and held her for a long while. "Thank you, God," I whispered as I stroked her beautiful chestnut hair.

As I stood on the cold kitchen floor, I began to realize I didn't hate Brittany but rather the choices she had made. Brittany wept while she held me tight. Her head was buried in my chest—something she had not done in many years.

My heart began to melt. She exposed her vulnerability. I hated the control Aldo asserted over Brittany. I hated the fact that I had felt powerless through the whole ordeal. But in that moment I knew that I loved Brittany more than words could say. I thanked God for bringing my daughter back to me.

Mike, Brittany, and I talked. Tears flowed. Hugs were shared. Even though my wounds were still fresh, I kept silent and calm. Great strides were made toward a genuine healing for us all.

We all agreed we would go and get the girls. Within four days, the correct paperwork was in hand. This was paperwork we had tried to gather on so many other occasions but were only met with Mexican bureaucracy, incorrect responses, and all at a snail's pace. Now Mike and Brittany were going down to Mexico with all the I's dotted and all the T's crossed. We could finally get the girls here legally.

God is so BIG and His timing is so perfect. This was the right moment in time. Everything fell into place. The first week of August 2005, Mike and Brittany drove to Juarez and picked up the girls. Aldo agreed to their move to the U.S.

Brittany was slow in revealing information about her ordeal. In mid-September 2006 she called and wanted to speak to me. Brittany was crying. She began, "Mom I just wanted to say that I'm sorry. I don't hate you and Dad. I just finished watching a show about children who were molested." I remained silent and let her speak. She continued, "Mom, I was molested when I was about 6 by a babysitter. I don't hate you, Mom. I was mad at you and Dad for not protecting me. I didn't even remember what happened until I watched this show tonight on TV."

My heart broke for her. I know firsthand the torture of molestation. Then she said, "Mom, that's why I left Mexico. Aldo had been accused of molesting three young teens while we were together. I know I told you the accusations weren't true, but I believe they were."

I knew Brittany had just hit on something. Aldo left with Brittany when she was young and innocent. After she bore two children, she had lost her innocence and appeal for Aldo. Aldo will always be the way he is, but my granddaughters did not have to live in that environment with him.

We talked on the phone for about an hour. Brittany shared with me that she was fearful that he would begin molesting his own daughters. Brittany loved them enough to make sure that would never happen. I could begin to see a glimmer of my precious daughter emerging from her heartfelt words. I began to realize that she had gone through hell herself.

Many times throughout the years I have searched for an apology from Brittany. Only now can it begin to unfold. We have a long way to go in healing our relationship, but it, too, will occur in time. My desire to protect my daughter from the evils of the world was viewed by her as overprotectiveness. I never thought that my own horrific experience as a teen-ager would ever return to haunt me, but now I know we cannot run from the past. It haunts us until we deal with it, even though we might try to suppress the memory, hoping against hope that it will fade into the background, never to be thought of again. Now the circle is complete. Hopefully the cycle will end here and not continue into future generations.

The road between Brittany and me is still filled with holes and pain, but we each are trying to find our way to a relationship of love and trust again. When she was small, we played a favorite game. I would pick her up and hold her close. Our eyes would meet. Slowly our faces would move together as if we were going to kiss. Instead, my nose would touch the soft skin on the tip of her nose. Very gently my nose would rub hers. I would say, "I love you, my special girl." Her eyes beamed with love.

Now I play that game with my granddaughter, April, age 4. She says, "Mema, can we play our special game?" With love, I caress her, stroke her hair, and we rub noses. Precious memories of Brittany return.

In conducting research for this book, I've also learned much about the peculiar relationship that develops between the child and one who lures a child away. Because most of our society thinks rationally, people have a tough time imagining what drives someone to entice a 15-year-old away from her parents and what motivates the child to stay.

Although a young person like Brittany may, in fact, walk away with someone such as Aldo, this usually only occurs after months of complex mind games. Aldo outskilled and outplayed Brittany; she was blindsided by his magical words and fanciful ideas. This sort of individual does not appear to be malevolent but rather appears to be a "normal" person. Aldo had a pleasant demeanor. He was helpful and very hospitable. He veiled his intentions in the disguise of a caring father and friend.

Someone who would entice a child away usually possesses superior reasoning skills. Aldo knew just what to say to build up Brittany's self-esteem and how to build her trust. The website for Missing and Exploited Children says such men single out teens that they sense are having problems at home. Brittany was a prime target because of her isolation from other teens. When we visited the restaurant, Club de Vela, Aldo would arrange the table seating so that he sat directly across from Brittany or would pull up a chair and sit next to her. In retrospect we believe that Aldo's conversations were aimed at casting doubt on our parenting skills and on highlighting our protective nature. More information about this type of situation can be found at *www.kidsave.com*. I hope that what I have shared might help even just one troubled teen. Because missing-persons cases are tragic and have commanded much media attention in our country, parents must be extremely vigilant about their children.

Lastly, as a note to the Christian, listen to the Holy Spirit's prompting when He tells you something is "just not right." Most likely He is warning you about an impending danger. Unfortunately I did not always heed His advice.

As I search my heart for my lessons learned, they are many. Sometimes the greatest blessings stem from the greatest pain. One lesson learned above all others is this: God loves us more than we can ever fathom.

To imagine a parent's love is to understand sacrifice. We did everything humanly possible to search for our daughter. We left no stone unturned. We spent our retirement funds. We almost let our marriage and our lives turn to shambles. "All for what?" you might ask. Unconditional love: no love in the world is like a parent's love.

I ask you, if a parent would do all that for his or her child, then how much more does God love us? God will move mountains for His children when they are lost, when they are broken, or when they need His touch. We all need a touch from our heavenly Father. Throughout this ordeal, I, too, became lost. My Father found me and healed my tattered soul. Thank you, Lord, for finding me and making me whole again.

Many times I thought God abandoned me because I could not see Him nor feel His presence. Just because we cannot see Him doesn't mean He cannot see us. He is forever watchful and faithful. He not only kept His eye on me, on many days He carried me when I thought I was walking alone.

During our early days in Bacalar, God taught me to be still. He, in His infinite wisdom, knew just how much I in the months ahead would need this gift. Stillness and rest are required to deliver us. In Psalm 37, David says, *Be still before the Lord and wait patiently for him . . . when men carry out their wicked schemes . . . refrain from anger and turn from wrath.* The Word is true. It has the power to heal. God's address is stillness. He is always there. All I had to do was be still. He wrapped His precious arms around me. In His arms I found His goodness.

As we move further away from this whole ordeal, I can begin to see the strides we have made. However, becoming parents again, as we now rear our granddaughters, has not been easy. While I remain a high-school English teacher, I have cut back on my extracurricular activities. Now my afternoons are filled with watching Marie Lou and April ride their bikes or playing Candy Land with them before dinner. Mike and I spend little time with our adult friends, but the rewards make everything worthwhile. A simple phrase from one of the girls saying, "You know what, Mema? I love you!" makes everything worth it. Aldo, who has started a new life outside of Cancun, rarely calls to check on his daughters. Time and prayer can heal our fragile souls.

Anger and hurt have been replaced by an undying love for our daughter. Brittany continues to make strides toward rearing the girls herself. She is working and visits the girls often.

Sometimes she keeps them for the weekend. She continues to struggle with keeping a steady job, running a household, and finding time for herself and the girls. Even though she is now 22, in many ways she is still a child. She finds great difficulty in making good decisions. Budgeting money and saving for the rent are still challenging tasks for Brittany. We pray that with time, Brittany will become a wonderful mother and a beautiful woman of God.

My butterflies visit often. God won't let me forget how special I am to Him. Recently He visited me in a dream. With the sky an azure blue, I stood in a field of beautiful wildflowers. Dozens of white butterflies hovered over the colorful vegetation. I felt His presence over me as I watched a white butterfly move from flower to flower. Over the first flower God said, "Manna! Food for the soul." Then, as the butterfly took the manna from the first flower and pollinated the next flower, I heard, "Someone needs a touch from Me." Over the next flower He said, "She needs forgiveness." From above I heard, "Love." "Reconciliation." The dream began to fade. But, oh, what a beautiful picture of how our Father works: through His children! He uses us to minister to each other; yet, it's just another miracle from Him. I am truly amazed at God's faithfulness.

Because of the growth we've experienced, I cannot imagine my life without our having undergone this ordeal. Time heals all wounds, but more importantly, God restores our souls. Thank You, Lord, for making me whole again.

And we know that in all things God works for the good of those who love him, who have been called according to his purpose (Rom. 8:28).

Photo Album

A team from Florida works on the clinic at Bacalar, Mexico.

The clinic under construction

José, Ninfa, Brittany, and Vanda stand in front of the clinic site. José and Ninfa's house is on right side.

Brittany and Ninfa inside Ninfa's home.

Vanda with a family in a small town outside Bacalar. They
stand outside the family's home.

More volunteer workers join in at the clinic site.

A team from Nederland, TX, clears land for the orphanage.

A church that Vanda, Mike, and team built in Chetumal

Inside a Chetumal church

Aldo and a pregnant Brittany in a park in Huatulco. Photo taken by Mike Guidry on his visit to Huatulco.

Vanda, Brittany, and Mike Terrell
Photo taken in June 2000.

Enjoy these other missions books

Rescue by Jean Phillips. Missionaries Jean Phillips and husband Gene lived through some of the most harrowing moments in African history of the last half century. Abducted and threatened with death, Jean and Gene draw on God's lessons of a lifetime.

_____Copies at $14.95=_____

The Man in the Green Jeep by Viola Palmer. Enjoy this captivating glance into children's lives and culture in Central America. See missionaries at work. Told through the eyes of a young boy whose life is changed by God's work on the mission field.

_____Copies at $12.95 = _____

Beyond Surrender by Barbara Singerman. Family ministers in Benin, West Africa—heart of voodoo worship. What keeps these servants there despite a frightening break-in, threatened abduction, and countless challenges?

_____Copies at $14.95 = _____

Servant on the Edge of History by Sam James. American missionaries feel called to remain in Vietnam during dangerous war era. God protects them despite countless narrow escapes. They return years later to see fruit borne during unthinkable period of turmoil.

_____Copies at $14.95 = _____

Add $4.00 postage and handling for first book, 50 cents for each additional book.

Shipping & Handling: _____

TX residents add 8.25% sales tax: _____

Total Enclosed
(check or money order) _____

Name _____

Address_____

City_____State_____Zip_____

Phone _____ Email _____

See address and other contact information on page 207.

To order additional copies
of *White Butterfly*
contact:

Hannibal Books
PO Box 461592
Garland, Texas 75046-1592
Call: 1-800-747-0738
hannibalbooks@earthlink.net
visit: www.hannibalbooks.com

09

Printed in the United States
91820LV00001B/7-54/A